Voices:
Past & Present

Voices:
Past & Present

THE TALKING STICK
VOLUME 25

A publication of the
Jackpine Writers' Bloc, Inc.
Menahga, Minnesota

ISBN: 978-1-928690-30-6

Send correspondence to sharrick1@wcta.net or
Jackpine Writers' Bloc, Inc., 13320 149th Avenue,
Menahga, Minnesota 56464.

Cover artwork contributed by Viola LaBounty
Managing Editors: Sharon Harris and Tarah L. Wolff
Copy Editors: Sharon Harris, Anne Morgan, Niomi Phillips,
        Marilyn Wolff, Tarah L. Wolff
Layout, Production and Cover Design: Tarah L. Wolff
Editorial Board: Marlys Guimaraes, Sharon Harris, Anne Morgan,
        Scott Stewart, Tarah L. Wolff

List of Contributors

List of Contributors

List of Contributors

List of Contributors

Co-Editor's Note - Sharon Harris
Editor's Choice: "When I Fell for Him" (p.51)
by Tarah L. Wolff

We have reached quite a milestone with Talking Stick 25. We want to thank the writers who first formed the Jackpine Writers' Bloc many years ago. This book seems enormous and has been a big project. We started talking about our twenty-fifth book several years ago, wondering how we could make it special. By reprinting some of our favorites from the earlier books, and combining past and present voices, we thought we could give an extra thanks to some of those founding members.

I have always been a poet and I have dabbled in short creative nonfiction. Each year, with these Talking Stick submissions, I have focused on the poems, searching for one that spoke to me. There was always one that I could choose as my Editor's Choice.

This year, there were certainly excellent poems that got to me (like "Farm Girl" by Cheryl Weibye Wilke on page 172, "Pregnancy" by Deb Schlueter on page 35, and "Hiding Places" by Jeanne Emrich on page 55). But this year, I was surprised to realize that my Editor's Choice had to be a fiction piece. "When I Fell for Him" by Tarah L. Wolff, my niece, is on page 51. This niece of mine does things I'd never do—I'd never rebuild a house and do all the electrical and plumbing myself, I'd never refinish furniture, I'd never crowd surf in a mosh pit at a heavy metal concert, and probably a few other things. I'd surely never jump off a bridge. But I can definitely remember the first touches, the tingles of falling in love, the awareness of each other—that magic that begins a relationship. The way that she described the jump from the bridge, the rush of the air, the feeling of hanging suspended over the water, the sense that time had stopped, the hearts beating together—I felt like I was right there.

"Everybody knows the fall is the best part."

Co-Editor's Note - Tarah L Wolff

Editor's Choice: "Dear Childhood Home:" (p.279)
by Margaret M. Marty

So, this is our 25th edition of The Talking Stick! And this is the 14th Talking Stick that I've designed from the front, all the way through, to the back of the book. What started as a learning curve (when I never had designed a book before) became a real aspect of who I am and turned into many other books I have had the opportunity to design. Throughout my last decade where I've seen so much change and loss in my own personal life, *The Talking Stick* and the Jackpine Writers' Bloc have offered an ever-present reminder of who I am, where I want to be and what I want to be doing, that I will ever remain so grateful for.

Sometimes we're stopped dead in our tracks by a piece, wondering if the writer had a direct line to a place in our own hearts and that, of course, is why we are readers. Finding out that someone out there shares such a direct memory or belief or experience so close to our own is the connection that reminds us why writing and reading are just so important.

And it is for that reason that I chose "Dear Childhood Home:" (p.279) by Margaret M. Marty this year, not only because it sparks in me memories passed to me from my own mom and aunt, but because it is a truly beautifully written poem. Like good fiction, this poem places you directly into a memory, able to smell and experience exactly what she is conveying. Being the kid myself who was called back to save the old farm place, she expressed something my own heart has been singing: "No wonder I was drawn,/like a magnet that won't be denied,/to spend the remainder of my life/on this hallowed piece of earth."

Just go read the whole poem; it is awesome.

Judges

Carson T. Gardner, Poetry Judge

Carson Gardner is a board-certified small-town family doctor and a founding member of the Jackpine Writers' Bloc. He left the practice of corporate medicine in 1999. Since then he and his wife Gail have been living and learning on the White Earth Ojibwe/Anishinaabe Reservation. Carson is now the medical director of the White Earth Nation Tribal Health Department and Reservation Ambulance Service. Carson has had poems and prose works published and he wrote lyrics for an album entitled *The Heron Smiled*. Carson is bear-clan, a cedar flute player, a traditionally-observant pipestone carver, a joyful dog rescuer, a perennial student of Ojibwe language, culture and spirituality, a compulsive storyteller and an ingenuous dreamer. (p.218)

Linda Henry, Creative Nonfiction Judge

Back in the day, Linda Henry helped launch the Jackpine Writers' Bloc and *The Talking Stick* as a way to give voice and ink to writers and artists. Her children's book, *The Cookie Garden*, illustrated by Dawn Rossbach (Beaver's Pond Press, 2015), was inspired during her time living in an earth home near Huntersville, Minnesota. Linda's author's website is **www.linda-henry.com**, where you can read her essays and occasional blog posts. (p.272)

Cynthia Ekren, Fiction Judge

A long-time member of the Jackpine Writers' Bloc, Cindie has had many stories and poems published in various *Talking Stick* volumes as well as *Artword Quarterly, Poetry Motel, Lake Country Journal* and other publications. As an English major, she has attended countless writing workshops over the years and taught writing to teens and at the Hope House in Bemidji. Now living in Florida, she is working on her novel set in Russia. (p.189)

Winners

Poetry: "Jim" (p.1) Meridel Kahl

Meridel retired in 2013 after forty-five years of teaching—the last twenty-seven at The College of St. Scholastica in Duluth, Minnesota. She loves every minute of her new life, especially the time she has to write. Her poems appear in *WritersRead* (Vol. 1, 2013), *The Thunderbird Review* (2014), *Amethyst and Agate: Poems of Lake Superior* (2015), and *The Talking Stick* (Vol. 24, 2015).

Creative Nonfiction: "The Word *Collage*, From the French, Means *to Glue*" (p.2) Sue Reed Crouse

Sue completed the Foreword Program, a two-year poetry apprenticeship, at the Loft Literary Center in Minneapolis in 2011. Her work appears in *The Talking Stick, Verse Wisconsin, Grey Sparrow, Earth's Daughters, Damselfly Press, Midway Journal, Gatherings: A Foreword Poetry Anthology, Aurorean* and *Unhinged Magazine*. Her manuscript, "One Black Shoe," was a finalist for the Backwaters Prize. She explores themes of grief and loss after the death of her daughter Laura. She lives with her husband, cat and "grumble" of pugs in Stillwater.

Fiction: "Delicate Tissue" (p.5) Paisley Kauffmann

Paisley and her husband live in Minneapolis. They enjoy weekend trips to Menahga to participate in their impressive writing community. She writes fiction with one of two pugs in her lap. Her short stories have been published in The *Talking Stick, The Birds We Piled Loosely*, and *The Writing Disorder*. Returning to school in 2013 in pursuit of a nursing degree put writing on hold, but she graduated in December and is back to writing. She takes Loft courses and participates in a writers' group.

Poetry 2nd place:
"Housewarming" (p.10) Peter Stein

Poetry Honorable Mention:
"Memorial Service" (p.74) Susan McMillan
"The Plain Things" (p.66) Mary Christine Kane
"Things Unsaid" (p.160) Larry Ellingson
"Pregnancy" (p.35) Deb Schlueter
"Buried in the Past" (p.88) Doris Lueth Stengel

Creative Nonfiction 2nd place:
"Cleaning John's House" (p.11) Cindy Fox

Creative Nonfiction Honorable Mention:
"Buoyancy" (p.37) Kristin Laurel
"Recipes" (p.283) Georgia A. Greeley
"Breakables" (p.183) Cheyenne Marco
"The Perfect Crime" (p.287) Mike Lein

Fiction 2nd place:
"No Place Like Home" (p.14) Cheyenne Marco

Fiction Honorable Mention:
"The Rehearsal" (p.275) Chet Corey
"Great Minnesota Get-Together" (p.99) Edis Flowerday
"Gold Bracelets" (p.249) Kathleen Lindstrom
"The Living Room" (p.219) P. Helen Kester

Foreward

The Jackpine Writers' Bloc was founded over twenty years ago by a group of people who loved to write and wanted to get published. They created the first volumes of *The Talking Stick*, starting out small and using various local publishers and editors. The book began with poems and stories from only the Park Rapids/Menahga area. Today, with our twenty-fifth book, we wish to celebrate those determined writers who first formed the JWB. Our book now includes writers from the whole state of Minnesota as well as writers who have a strong connection to Minnesota.

At first, the group published two books per year, which later changed to one. Now we accept submissions for three genres and we give cash prizes. The book is larger now too. The goal of The Jackpine Writers' Bloc is still simple—we want to encourage and publish Minnesota writers.

We contacted as many of the earlier members as we could. Here are the bios of some of them along with the page numbers of their poems and stories, reprinted with their permission from some of the earlier *Talking Stick* books. Look for the large asterisks that mark their pages.

Featured in this book are the three judges plus the following writers:

Beth Diane Bradley (p.31) Beth mainly wrote poetry when she joined the JWB in the early 2000s. But one day she brought a short piece of humorous prose to a meeting. Members liked it and suggested she write essays. Her collection of essays can be found at **www.boomersbliss.areavoices.com**. Her work has also been featured in *Area Woman Magazine, High Plaines Reader, The Huffington Post,* and on Prairie Public's statewide radio network. She has moved back to her native Fargo, but can see Minnesota from her kitchen window.

Angele (Burlingame) Hartell (p.278) Angele is employed with the State of Minnesota in workforce development and, in that capacity, routinely writes a regional e-news publication. Creative writing efforts include successful starts in developing three books, the titles of which will remain secret because they are so catchy. She has thirteen more catchy titles and great intentions of starting those as well. This is the life of the stalled writer, waiting for retirement as an opportunity to write full time. The JWB provided impetus and inspiration for early writing efforts, including a poem published in *The Talking Stick*, and an essay published in *Lake Country Journal*.

Deane Johnson (p.265) Deane has lived in Park Rapids, Minnesota, for thirty-six years and is a retired family physician. He and his wife Jill collaborated on her book *Little Minnesota: 100 Towns Around 100,* and a forthcoming book about World War II veterans from these small towns. Deane wrote and photographed *The Best of Itasca: A Guide to Minnesota's Oldest State Park,* and was one of the original members of JWB. The early days with the group helped him shape and understand others' response to his writing.

Norma Thorstad Knapp (p.239) Norma grew up in western North Dakota. Her children's book *Missing My Best Friend* was published in June 2011 and is now listed on the National Bereavement Resource List. Knapp's second book *Scoria Roads* was nominated for a 2016 Minnesota Book Award in the Memoir and Creative Nonfiction category. Today Norma lives in Alexandria, Minnesota. Her days are full with writing, traveling, and hospice bereavement work. **www.normaknapp.com**. The JWB helped her get past her self-doubts, insecurities and aimlessness that were holding her back. She was reminded to write through her projects. The JWB gave her challenges and accountability.

Florence Witkop (p.49) Florence was one of the original members of the Jackpine Writers' Bloc. She has been writing for more years than many people have been alive! Some of her writing is done for money, sometimes for fun, including with the Jackpine Writers' Bloc. Information about Florence and her books and some short fiction can be found on her website **www.florencewitkop.com**.

Eric Wolff (p.139) Eric enjoys spending time with his family, as well as selling real estate, hunting, and fishing.

Voices:
Past & Present

Jim

I made soup on that cold spring day.
I sautéed garlic with red pepper flakes
dropped one-inch pieces
of bright orange squash
into hot broth.

Perhaps as I seasoned the kettle
with sweet basil and thyme—
perhaps before or after that—
a man I once loved
died in a quiet room
two hundred miles away.

When I heard of his death,
ache spread
like oil in my chest—
not so much from tender memories
nor our painful parting,

but from the familiar shock
that whenever someone dies,
the Earth neither gives notice
nor pauses in its spinning.

It does not change daylight to dusk,
does not—even for an instant—
turn a pot of simmering soup to ice.

Creative Nonfiction/*1st Place*/Sue Reed Crouse

The Word *Collage*, From the French, Means *to Glue*

She was sitting on the curb outside the coffee shop with her friends when I arrived, balancing a 2'x3' piece of plywood against her knees. She stood up, hoisted the board, which I suspected she'd retrieved from the construction dumpster nearby, and made her way to the car. Bolted to the front of the plywood was a metal circuit box, out of which a variety of colorful wires sprouted. A segmented conduit flopped over the top and a chipped, plastic plate framed an oily light switch.

"I hope you're taking that thing to your apartment," I snapped at my artistic twenty-year-old daughter. "I don't want it lying around the basement."

"I'm going to make something very cool out of it," Laura retorted, her chin high.

A month later she was dead, having fallen through a damaged portion of walkway on the Arcola High Bridge. We cleaned out her apartment and there was the old board, painted blue-grey. She had bolted a black picture frame to the front, painted the light switch gold and added a surreal picture of a black rose, suspended in sooty air. The piece was clearly unfinished, propped against an end-table (also saved from a dumpster) and surrounded by coffee cans filled with bits of wire, metal washers and peculiar hardware. She obviously envisioned some marvelous industrial vibe, but I would never know.

During the ensuing year, walking felt unfamiliar and treacherous as I no longer trusted the ground beneath my feet. Nothing about my life or myself felt familiar or survivable. Each day I looked at the board, now leaning against the wall in my office. It had become a symbol of my grief and regret.

One day, as I thought about William Stafford's poem,

detailing the disparate contents of his journal, I curled the wires from the board around a pencil to look like morning-glory vines, and placed paper flowers on the ends. A few days later, I glued some black stones to the board. Then, a passage from the book Laura had been reading, *The Heart of Understanding* by Thich Nhat Hanh. Then, a chunky flower she'd drawn with green crayon when she was a little girl. Before long, I had my first collage, a fusion of Steampunk and Bereaved Mom.

Until then, I had buried myself in a frantic repertoire of activity in the desperate search for solace. I obsessively read and wrote poetry. I created an elaborate garden with flowers bearing her name. I found meaningful volunteer work. I made quilts. While all of these activities eased the agony a bit, it was work on the rescued board that gave me courage to slow down and consider what some call the "new normal." Something about the process and the result seemed much greater than the sum of all these modest parts and the time spent selecting and attaching them. As Stafford wrote that his journal contained *mean things, fishhooks, barbs in your hand,* also, *space for Alaska,* so the collage held bouquets of eight-penny nails—nail-heads painted like daisies—and space for my Alaska-dwarfing sorrow. I found myself saving the onion bag because of its intricate red weave. I gathered fallen hollyhock blossoms because they resembled butterflies. I pried rusted washers from the heat-softened asphalt during my walks. I began to see possibility in what seemed worthless and felt compelled to give these objects a strange, new life.

In the seven years since Laura's death, I've made hundreds of collages. I've sewn leaves and frayed rope to paper. A cache of sticky lollipop sticks I found in her apartment became flower stems. The tiniest scraps of paper upon which she'd jotted a phone number or note became clouds above mountains torn from pages of poetry. I shredded a copy of her death certificate and wove the strips with floral ribbon. Some of the collages shout with rage and agony. I've burned photographs, hacked up paper with razor blades and scribbled pencil-breaking, page-ripping profanity, all of which have been set into collage. Others are lovely and quiet, containing poetry and watercolor. Bits of her clothing. Wire. Crushed flowers encased in tulle and scribble-sewn to paper. Soil from her grave.

At some point, it occurred to me that collage was simply a metaphor for what I had to do in order to continue. I had to take the shards of my life and somehow glue them together in a new way. Collage demonstrated that I could integrate her death into my life and survive. I didn't have to *move on* or *let go* or any of the troubling platitudes that are often directed at the bereaved. I could hold on to everything and transform it into art, which offered me a new way to relate to my daughter.

Laura's collection of rusty hardware is slowly being incorporated—along with my own found objects, poetry and art—into a collection that honors and celebrates her life and my grief process. Following Laura's lead with the discarded board, I've developed, through collage, a conduit through which we both can travel, each toward the other.

Fiction/*1st Place*/Paisley Kauffmann

Delicate Tissue

The electronic ring pierces the dark, cozy bedroom. Robert smacks his lips and clears his throat before answering. Penny combats against a sense of dread and refuses to open her eyes.

"Hello?" Robert says. The question in his voice indicates it is an unknown number.

"This is he," he says and listens. He jerks to a sitting position.

She opens her eyes.

Holding the phone to his ear, Robert gets out of bed. He struggles, awkwardly with one hand, to get both legs threaded into his black pants.

She sits up. Mildly and secretly annoyed, she knows the call has something to do with one of his kids.

"Have you contacted his mother?" he asks, and says, "Okay. I'm on my way." He tosses the phone onto the bed and walks into the bathroom.

Reluctantly, she peels back the down comforter and stands in the bathroom door with her arms wrapped over her chest. "Robert? What's going on?"

He splashes water on his face, pats dry with a towel, and says, "It's Bobby. He's in the hospital. He dove into a pool and broke his neck."

"Oh, my god," she says. "I'll go with you."

He nods.

She, anticipating the presence of the ex-wife, washes her face and briefly considers applying a few dabs of makeup. Although Robert and Margaux divorced many years ago, she feels in constant competition with her, a successful lawyer with great skin and long legs. Robert, ready to leave, jingles his keys from hand to hand.

Instead of foundation and mascara, she pulls on her most flattering jeans and slips lip gloss into her back pocket.

In the car, Robert races through the fresh snow, fishtailing and sliding. She grips the armrest and fights the urge to complain.

"What pool?" she asks, contemplating the subzero temperature.

"I don't know," he says. "A hotel? Don't kids still have hotel parties?"

She shrugs. Robert often asks her what kids are up to these days. Their age difference is significant, but she is not privy to the antics of teenagers. She worked two jobs through high school; teenage pastimes have always been a mystery.

Under florescent lights, she jogs to keep up with Robert's long strides through the hospital corridors. She regrets not applying any makeup. Florescent lighting reflects in green undertones against her blond hair and washes out her fair skin.

Margaux is standing at the nurses' station gesticulating and demanding information in her authoritative, strident voice. Robert places his hand on Margaux's back and she collapses into his arms. Her face is drained of color, and Penny feels perversely satisfied with the pallor replacing her normally rich, olive tones.

"He's in bad shape," Margaux repeats into Robert's shoulder.

Robert ushers Margaux under his arm and signals for Penny to follow to a row of plastic chairs near the vending machines.

"Sit with her," Robert instructs, and walks away.

Penny hesitates, but does as she is told.

Margaux, wrapped in an expensive-looking shawl, smashes a tired tissue to her nose. "They say he may not walk again."

Shaking her head, Penny considers touching Margaux's hand or shoulder, but any gesture she attempts seems contrived.

"Boys," Margaux says, trying to unfold the damp tissue. "They do such careless things."

Grateful for something to do, Penny stands and says, "I'll find you some more Kleenex." She reaches for a box of economy-brand tissues behind the empty nurses' station. Robert, down the hall with the doctor, is covering his face with his hand and shaking his head. The doctor reaches out and squeezes Robert's shoulder. As Penny grasps the tissue box, the fluorescent light fires off the facets of her engagement ring, a large diamond flanked with baguettes set in a platinum band. It is the biggest diamond she has ever seen, and she loves the attention it attracts. She returns to the seat next to Margaux, and rapidly pulls three stiff tissues from the box.

"Thank you," Margaux says.

"This changes everything," Margaux chants. "Everything will be different."

Penny pulls a tissue from the box and folds it against her knee.

"He is never going to walk. They don't know if he can even breathe on his own," Margaux says and chokes on a sob.

Penny squeezes her fingers against the ring and it cuts into her flesh.

"He will have to live at home with one of us. At least until—"

Robert returns and stands over them.

"What have they told you?" Margaux asks.

Robert blinks at her.

"Please, please tell me he's going to be okay," Margaux begs.

Robert drops into the chair and Margaux envelops him in her shawl.

Penny, an invisible, superfluous observer, stands and walks away. Outside, the night is brittle with unquestionable clarity. A group of nurses are gathered in a susurrant smoking circle. Penny approaches and asks no one in particular for a cigarette. There is a long, uncomfortable pause before a young nurse, younger than herself, holds out a white, papery cigarette. Without having to ask, she is handed a lighter.

Penny walks around the hospital and resists articulating the one question bubbling to the surface. It is an unforgivable and obstinate question: *Why is this happening to me?* A bus pulls up to the curb with a hydraulic squeal. The fumes sting her nose. She walks towards the bus and the doors fold open like a magic portal to another dimension.

"You getting on?" the bus driver asks.

Penny drops her cigarette in the snow, considers the question, and says, "No."

"Are you sure?"

She steps back. "I'm sure."

The doors snap shut and the bus bounces away from her.

Her feet, wet and cold, begin to ache. She pulls the rough tissue from her coat pocket and wipes her running nose. The streets leading away from the hospital invite her to escape down their unmarked, snow-covered sidewalks illuminated by the moon. Mirages of fairy-tale endings pixelate at the end of each city block. Her fingers are numb, and she checks for her ring. It is still there noosed around her finger. Slipping it off, she stuffs it into the pocket of her jeans.

At the hospital entrance, three yellow taxi cabs pump exuberant exhaust into the frigid air. Penny searches her coat pockets for money. She has seventeen dollars and forty-two cents. It may be enough to get her to the airport. She decides to buy a ticket to wherever the next available flight is headed. Climbing into the first cab, she rouses the driver from a nap, and says, "Airport, please."

The cab driver sits up in his seat. "Luggage?"

"No luggage."

He shifts the car into drive, and they lurch forward.

"Going somewhere warm?" the cab driver asks, glancing at her in the rearview mirror.

"I don't know, maybe," she answers his reflection. "Where are you from?"

"Iraq," he says, accelerating and merging onto the freeway. "But you don't want to go there."

"I suppose not."

"It's nice here," he says. "Too cold in the winter, but the other seasons are good."

The streetlights flash by in regular beats.

"Are you traveling alone?" he asks.

"No," she answers. "I'm engaged. My fiance is meeting me in . . ."

She starts to cry. Reaching for the tissue, she recalls her mother handing her two tissues and instructing her to cry until they were both used up. After that, it was time to deal with the problem and move on with life.

The cab driver clicks on the blinker towards the airport exit.

"You can take me back to the hospital."

The driver nods and turns off the blinker.

Shoulders heaving, she cries until the tissue crumbles apart.

The driver rolls up to the exact location they departed from, shifts into park, and says, "You can sit in here for a while longer. It's a slow night."

She nods.

"Do you mind if I turn on some music?"

She shakes her head.

Arabic music fills the space. Quick tempos, sliding scales, and unfamiliar soft words punctuated with glottal utterances.

Closing her eyes, she escapes.

"Miss?" The driver wakes her.

She startles back into her reality.

"I'm sorry, but my shift is over."

She wraps her coat around her and reaches into her pocket for the seventeen dollars. "I only have, well, less than twenty dollars."

He waves it away.

Penny gets out of the warm, fragrant cab and squints at the white and red lights of the hospital entrance. She pulls the ring from her pocket and slips it on. Gazing at her hand, the ring encircles her finger like a constrictor.

Under the scrutiny of florescent lights, she returns to find Robert sitting with his elbows on his knees and his face buried in his palms.

Standing in front of him, she places her hands on his shoulders.

He wraps his arms around her waist, and says, "You're here."

"I'm here," she says.

Poetry/*2nd Place*/Peter Stein

Housewarming

Life is so simple
when your house is on fire

All there is to do is stand on the front lawn
and watch the flames as your home
shows its full potential turned kinetic

The lumpy couch with a stain on one cushion, a hole in the
        other
The toaster that only toasted one side
The laptop with a sticky keyboard and dead battery,
files all stored remotely
The dining table scuffed and wobbly
will be replaced and scuffed and wobbly soon enough

If you're lucky
you manage to escape unscathed
with a camping chair, cup holder
on the arm, and a beer from your late fridge
to enjoy a cool evening,
the warm flicker of orange,
a mouthful of s'mores

Creative Nonfiction/ *2nd Place*/Cindy Fox

Cleaning John's House

My brother John will be discharged from the hospital tomorrow, a welcome ten-day reprieve before his next round of chemo treatment. Good news. But his doctor doesn't know he's releasing him to a dirty house, a filthy breeding ground where infection could attack his weakened immune system. So on this Sunday morning, I, along with our other siblings, gather at his bachelor abode, armed with cleaning supplies to sanitize his house.

The petrified air is heavy with the unhappy mix of cigarette smoke and Asian ladybug beetles. The kitchen table is buried under mounds of bills and catalogs and junk mail. Cookbooks, dirty dishes, and bags of stale bread and cookies litter the counter top.

Yet the emptiness overwhelms me; it feels like a presence I have to push through.

Candles are lit and an apple-cinnamon fragrance sweetens the air and the sour chores before us. But where to begin? My sisters gather around the kitchen table to decide who will clean which room. I hear "bathroom," fake deafness, and step closer to the living room.

Ladybugs crunch below my feet. More hibernate on windowsills and between folds of the curtains. A massive refuge of upturned bodies blanket the floor behind furniture. Where's the vacuum cleaner? Brother Ed finds a vacuum in the basement, but it's dead on arrival. Back from his truck, he returns with a Shop-Vac that rat-tat-tats while sucking up ladybugs like an anteater.

Like every year, swarms of ladybugs arrive in October, the same month John was diagnosed with cancer. I imagine him saying to hell with fighting to keep them outside his house. He had a bigger battle to win.

I stand before the entertainment stand, a chaos of clutter stuffed on shelves and on top. I hadn't realized John was such a hoarder. Cassette and VHS tapes are scattered in and around the stand that has no VCR. Why does he save them? A vintage tube television is unplugged and sits on the stand's big shelf, perhaps for appearance sake. What else would one put in that big open space?

Family photographs in frames with broken legs lean against knickknacks he has acquired from his travels abroad. Cobwebs drape between two Asian wood dolls and cover their heads like hairnets. I dab my dust cloth on their delicate faces and gently remove the lacy veil from their shoulders and slender arms, crossed as if in prayer.

Many years ago he bought the dolls in Indonesia where he worked building a golf course. He was a high-roller then, his pockets filled with money he earned overseas that wasn't taxed by the IRS. He had maids who washed his clothes, cooked his meals, and a chauffeur who drove him to work. Back in Minnesota, he built a log house two miles from our hometown. A house that hasn't had maid service until now.

I wipe grime off each tape, book, and framed photograph before stacking them on the floor and carefully move his souvenirs to an open space on the kitchen table. I don rubber gloves and fill my water pail with a double dose of Lysol which promises 99.9% disinfecting powers and a "sparkling lemon essence" scent. The powerful smell stings my eyes and nose. I wonder what the vapors are doing to my mucous membranes. Will they cause cancer without proper ventilation? The bottle's warning label is in fine print that can only be read with a magnifying glass. Too late now. The damage, if any, has been done. It's January in Minnesota. Too cold to open the windows. Windows. I groan when I look at the six-foot panes dribbled with beetle juice and promise myself I'll get to them later.

The entertainment stand is now barren but for dark imprints in the dust. I drag my saturated paper towel across the shelf. Dust, layered with grease, rolls around like mouse turds. One more time. More turds. Longer turds. I pour Lysol full strength onto a fresh towel and scrub until my arm quivers. I don't worry about damaging the fake wood finish which has been glued onto wafer board. The next shelf flops up and down with each swipe of my cloth as it's missing a support peg. It dawns on me then. Why don't I pull out the shelves to clean them? I look around to see if anyone has witnessed my stupidity. Nope. But I hear screams from the bedroom, then laughter. One of my sisters found a fake hand behind a dresser, no doubt one of John's pranks used to scare his Halloween weekend visitors.

That was two months ago—late October when he still felt good enough to laugh. When perhaps denial cloaked over him like a witch's cape, its upturned collar protecting him from the vampire's bite of fear. Before the burning sting of radiation. Before the poisonous drips of chemo into his veins. When he still felt normal.

The girls are still giggling, but there's nothing funny in front of me. Only a cheap particle board stand with nicks and scratches and rickety shelves with no electronics to play his old tapes that were all the rage when he was young and rich and healthy.

Five hours later, we're exhausted but the house is squeaky clean and a lovely lemony scent lingers after the candles are blown out. I load the car with John's laundry and will return tomorrow with fresh sheets for his bed. I will fix the wobbly shelf and set up my old VCR I couldn't bear to throw away when DVDs made it obsolete. I will slide in his *White Fang* tape about a wolf that beat the odds. I only hope the television works when I plug it in.

Fiction/*2nd Place*/Cheyenne Marco

No Place Like Home

Nelle sat at the kitchen table with an empty can of Coke. She held it in front of her, twisting it so shards of light glittered on the cupboard faces. The rays were the purest white-blue she'd ever seen. Was it the aluminum? Maybe some tin had been mixed in with the batch. She remembered when her father would burn the trash out at the farm. After a construction job, he would throw scraps of tin in the fire so she could watch the flames turn white-blue. Nothing seemed more honest than the flames waving in the pit, looking like the sky reflected in a heaving lake.

For this reason—and the twelve other reasons she'd found in memories prompted by the nail polish-red lettering and lip print on the rim—she placed the can in the pyramid of cans she had stacked on her table. It looked like a Christmas tree, and it almost reached the ceiling. She was running out of room. Her collection of favorite fast food napkins claimed the top of the fridge, and the empty butter containers were stacked up in the corner. Old sponges created a mosaic on the counter top. The kitchen had been used up, and she couldn't bear the thought of her next can tree having to be erected in the living room. Food and beverage stuff went in the kitchen. VHS tapes, throw pillows, clocks, and rugs went in the living room.

Everything had a place.

The tree still had enough room for six or seven more cans. If she didn't drink any more pop this week, she could push the problem off until a design epiphany struck her and God would give her space out of thin air for all the cans she'd keep.

A knock on the door distracted her from her fixation. It was the light, regular rap she expected at 11 a.m. on every day but Sunday. Sammy rarely strayed more than five minutes from his delivery schedule. No one dared to try to slow him down. In addition to the mail route, he ran the bar, and anyone who made his day job hell got weak drinks at night.

"Good morning, Nellie Bell." Sammy held out three letters, keeping his eyes focused on Nelle and showing no interest in the house. The whole town knew about the house, but they had as much consideration for it as they did for black holes: scary but not a real threat. "Three deliveries. Somebody sure is popular today."

"I'm not even sure I know three people." She laughed and took the letters.

"Well, one of 'em's the reunion, of course. I've been handing them out to half the people in town. Myself included."

"Ah, Sammy boy. There were only twenty-two kids in our graduating class and half of them left. Stop exaggerating."

"It feels like a lot of people. The town feels downright overcrowded some days."

Nelle snickered. "Sure does, don't it?"

"It sure does." He nodded, and the bill of his cap leapt up a bit, giving a nod of its own.

Fearing a little too much orange juice in her screwdriver, Nelle smiled and stepped back from the door. "Thanks, Sam."

"See you later, Nelle."

She examined the three envelopes: her bank statement, her Visa bill, and what had to be the reunion invite. It looked like Lisa's handwriting, but she had a hard time believing Lisa would address twenty-two envelopes and not make Dave do it.

Nelle slid her fingernail under the seam of the envelope, trying to cause as little damage as possible. Letters needed to go back in their envelopes for easier filing. The invitation was a disappointment, typed in the same boring font of a city citation. The blocky text looked as though it may have been created by a typewriter. In this old town, it wasn't a bad guess. The purple wildcat logo at the top winked at her, as if trying to charm her out of her disparagement.

The twenty-year reunion would be held two Saturdays from today. A two-week notice bordered on being rude, but she'd come to expect little from her former classmates. In fact, she didn't imagine that many would even come. They'd all forgotten where they'd come from so quickly. After graduation, most of them moved. Rhonda went to New York, and Brian—her dear, sweet Brian—ended up in Minneapolis. Half of them came back, a detail that she twisted delightedly around her fingers like an errant thread. What a silly waste. They'd gone searching for something she'd known was here all along.

Nelle scampered up the steps to the guest bedroom, where she kept half her clothes and all her quilts and comforters. She sat on the bed, which was laden with blankets, and felt as though she were on a cloud. Racks lined the perimeter of the room, and she stared at each one in turn. She placed her pointer finger in the dimple of her chin as she contemplated. The black dress she'd worn to her uncle's funeral looked appropriately shiny, but she wondered if Beth would recognize it and make a morbid joke. Nelle tossed her blonde hair, like a stallion's mane, in protest. There was the skirt she'd worn to her cousin's wedding, the blue suit she'd gotten half off, and the green halter with the duck sewn into the bottom hem. She admired every one, but none were quite right

She slid off the bed and reached for the dress tucked between her christening dress and her graduation gown. Purple gossamer flowed to the floor, rustling over the satin beneath. The gossamer was wrapped just above the waist and flowed out in an inverted V. Nelle remembered the name of the shade: royal. Not lilac. Not plum. Not mauve. Royal. A silver-studded belt divided the lower flood of fabric from the tight, minimal top, which cut dangerously low and twisted up into braided spaghetti straps.

Her prom dress had always been her favorite, and she imagined getting married one day in a white replica.

As she slipped the straps off the hanger, she thought about Tom Sayers and his wife in Duluth. They came back for the holidays to visit his parents. Two weeks probably wouldn't be enough notice for him to take off work and drive across the state. His wife probably had something planned for him anyway. Drowning on the Great Lakes or food poisoning at a new restaurant. That's how he seemed to spend his time, according to Facebook anyway. Nelle felt sorry for him. Kimmy, Steve, Simon, and Emily were in the same boat, just on different lakes. She felt sorry for them too.

The dress still fit. The strap still rubbed against her exposed clavicle. She extended her circle of pity to those women who probably couldn't fit in their prom dresses anymore: Shannon, Darla, Myra. Nelle stood on her tiptoes and grabbed the shoebox from the shelf on top of the rack. She retrieved the silver beaded bracelet and matching necklace and earrings that slept inside. As she slipped the bracelet on her wrist, the shimmering beads became the tears of all those women who had converted years into pounds.

Next, she went to the bathroom and painted her eyes purple and twisted her hair up into a raining fountain. She darted back to the guest room, ducked down, and grabbed another shoebox tucked underneath the rack. Inside was a pair of strappy stilettos. A dark stain outlined where her foot had settled twenty years ago. The silver didn't shine as brightly and the fabric looked puckered. She slid her foot in the shoe and wrapped the straps around her ankle.

And she was Cinderella, the very princess she had been twenty years ago.

She twirled and imagined herself gliding over the gym floor. Twenty years hadn't made that much of a difference. She couldn't be touched by time, couldn't be forced through space. Sheltered by her soda cans and insulated by her blankets, she had preserved herself. She had saved herself for this moment.

Nelle completed her spin and lowered herself onto the bed. She sat on the edge of her cloud, dangling above her world. She kept her back straight, smoothed the material of her dress over her lap, and waited there for two Saturdays.

Poetry/Deborah Rasmussen

Test

The classroom was quiet as a cornfield
that first day,
disturbed by nothing
but her steps
past columns of country children

waiting.

She felt them watch
as she rounded the oak desk,
wore its finish farther down
with one slow finger,
faced them,
and, in no hurry,
sat.

She was herself a child of the country

so when she opened the drawer,
found inside a snake
carefully coiled,
recently dead,
she simply
closed it.
Began the day.

The room breathed.

Outside
quiescent cornfields breathed too,
stirring fresh life
into expectant stalks.

Creative Nonfiction/Sharon Harris

Knowing Mother

I am determined. Today I will get the answers I want. I have asked her time and time again. Today she will finally answer me. I have asked her many times about her boyfriends before Dad. I think it would be fun to know. Dad has been gone five years now. I have this book called *The Story of a Life* with questions about her life and I can throw in a few more—she won't know if I do.

We sit in the old farmhouse kitchen. It is hot. I have bullied her into getting an air conditioner, finally. With that on full blast and several fans, the house is almost bearable. We sit at the oval table. It is only the second table I ever remember in this house. The old larger rectangular one—where the four of us ate our meals all those years—was replaced by this smaller oval one when we girls got married. Then they had room for the portable dishwasher and TV—and later her viewer when her eyesight diminished.

The smell of cat urine wafts to me sometimes and the mustiness comes up from the basement. The odor of Friskies cat food is strong too. Mother sits, arms on the table, waiting. Her hair is wild, like she has not combed it today—or maybe finger-combed it too many times. When she becomes stubborn and won't answer me—her teeth clench and her jaw is set and that chin is all pinched up and trembling. Her eyes narrow and she won't look at me.

No matter how much I ask her, she is still a stranger to me. I wonder what makes her tick, what makes her glad to get up in the morning—what drove her all those years on the farm to plant the flowers, plant the garden, milk the cows, cook the meals, sew for us two girls—what she remembers of her life and what she really thinks about life in general.

All around this house are wooden things they have built. A shelf on the wall is a mirror from an old dresser. Knickknacks sit there like they have for fifty years, laden with dust. A thing set down in an old farm house may remain for decades. Glued-together figurines, once broken, painstakingly repaired, line the shelves.

Her face is the softest thing I've ever felt, like flannel or a baby blanket. Soft and fragile, oh, so fragile, like life itself can be. Someday she will be gone, this lady in her early nineties. I fear she will die without me really knowing her. I won't know her feelings, her memories, her likes and dislikes. I do know that she believes in being dignified and doesn't like anything that is silly or frivolous. But she has forgotten so much over the last few years that it is frightening. She remembers her childhood, and I know darned well she remembers her old boyfriends, but she does not remember much of the time since Dad's stroke. Sadly, she is also forgetting many things from their married years. I think she is frightened by it too and angered. She hates to admit she can't remember something. I think when we mention things that she doesn't remember, she sometimes doesn't let on. I think she is very clever about covering up when she doesn't remember something.

She sits near me now, upright and rigid, ramrod-straight.

"Okay, Mother. Are you ready? We're going to go through this book now, question by question. And if you get tired and want to call it a day, you have to tell me."

"I suppose, if we have to." Her fingers scratch at some imaginary piece of old food stuck to the table's surface. She has told me several times now that the book should be called *The Life of a Story*, since Story is her maiden name. She is nothing if not witty, this mother of ours.

I began with the questions about her grandparents. Amazingly, she remembered all the names, their brothers and sisters, etc. Of course, I didn't know if she was right or not, but it sounded good. I recorded everything.

"Tell me about some of your earliest memories of growing up on the farm." And she did, complete with describing all the old homestead buildings and their placement in the yard—the old house and later the new house—and even remembered cat names and dog names.

"We built a new house and the old house was pulled away by our team of horses. Part of it was made into a chicken coop. Part of it became a granary. Part of it became a playhouse for us kids."

She described all the rooms in the old house and the new house, the location of the bedrooms, etc. I knew she was right about all this. We had recently been to see that house she grew up in, newly remodeled, with a new family living in it.

I moved her on through the questions, childhood memories, school memories, thoughts of her dad and mother, sister and brother. She was careful, grudging of the information she gave, but she did really well. She could tell me facts, but she was guarded about her feelings, reluctant to share them. Her mother had died when my mom was only five. She told me she had only one memory of her mother—sitting on a stool in the kitchen while her mother took a splinter out of her finger.

Then was my chance. "And when you got a little older, who did you first go out on a date with?"

A stony silence. Her jaw set, her teeth clenched, and that chin of hers was so tight that it trembled violently. She used to tell me that this subject wasn't important—people I wouldn't know anyway.

Now she said, glancing my way with (I swear) a small smirk on her lips, "I don't remember."

Poetry/Sandra Howlett

What I Learned From My Mother

I learned to fish from my mother,
how to set up a tent,
to drink hot cocoa before bed
to stay warm in your sleeping bag

I learned to sing from my mother,
to love musicals, to cry at episodes
of the Brady Bunch, the importance
of good friends and good times

I learned to dance from my mother,
how to do the Charleston and the Can-Can,
to tap dance, and learned that
you are never too old to clog

I learned to survive from my mother,
how to rely on a man until you couldn't,
how to climb a mountain, unclog
garbage disposals, and dispose of rats

I learned to drink from my mother,
how to start happy hour at 3 p.m.
every day, how to buy gallon
bottles of Gallo wine so you won't run out

Creative Nonfiction/Cindy Fox

Everything Will Be Okay

The phone screamed in the dark of night, jolting me out of bed. My heart pounded and the first thing that popped into my head was: *Who died?* The voice on the phone was calm, the message foreboding. My brother Ron lay motionless on a hospital bed. We needed to come right away. There wasn't much time.

Their first time on an airplane, my parents' hands gripped the armrests. Mother's swollen knuckles were riddled with rheumatoid arthritis. Dirt and grease embedded Dad's fingernails, the creases on his hands stamping his life as a farmer. The plane lifted off the tarmac and their eyes turned to me, desperate and earnest. I assured them the lurch in their stomachs would go away, that everything would be okay.

I followed my parents into the cold and clammy hospital room, the walls painted a sickly green. Ron lay unresponsive while artificial hands from beeping machines covered his mouth and poked his body.

I stared at his thirty-two-year-old face, no longer the gawky student pictured in his high school yearbook with the silly quotation, "He studies, but he's perfectly normal." I cringed at my insensitivity back in school. While he had his nose in a book, I walked around with my nose up in the air and pretended I didn't know him.

The doctor explained to my parents what had happened to their son. An aneurysm, a bulging, weak artery, ruptured on his brain. A condition which was irreversible and un-recoverable. A ventilator breathed for him and kept his heart and other organs alive, but not his brain. A flat elec-troencephalogram showed no brain activity.

My brother, who was a brain in school, was declared brain-dead.

The doctor asked if they had any questions. The blunt truth, the shock of it all, left them dazed. Dad, with his hands in his pockets, shrugged his shoulders like he always did when he was nervous. Usually the outspoken one, he turned to Mom to ask the questions. Her eyes, washed out with grief and fatigue, looked at him and then down at the floor. She said nothing.

The doctor left and Dad nonchalantly said, "He looks like he's sleeping." Shocked at his apathetic tone, I quickly dismissed it as his way of coping with denial.

As delicately as possible, I said, "Ron can't hear or say anything."

Ignoring my comment, they stroked his arms and crooned, "Everything will be okay."

A person who says someone thinks with their heart instead of their head has never been in a hospital room with a brain-dead person. The heart cannot think if there is no brain. But my parents, who feared the worst for their child, thought with their hearts and told him once again that everything would be okay.

They spoke about miracles and how others had come out of coma and lived productive lives. Clearly, they didn't understand Ron was not in a vegetative state or simply unconscious. I didn't want to dwindle any hope they held for their firstborn son. I was a parent, too. I said nothing.

My father, keeping his pain to himself, paced the room and then left to smoke a cigarette. At first, I thought I should accompany him. Would he get lost in the maze of hallways? Would he know which button to push in the elevator? Would he know to smoke outside? Or would he sit in the lobby and flick ashes into his pant cuff like he did at home when no ashtray was nearby? Instead, I turned to my mother whose slumped shoulders were draped in sadness.

She pinched her lips to stop them from trembling. She let out a haggard breath, wiped her eyes, and said, "He's too young to die."

Die. The word cut me deep when I thought of my own children. I wrapped my arms around her, comforted by her scent and soft body that had consoled my childhood tears. We cried together, sharing the deep-down agony of impending loss of a child that only a mother can feel.

There was a time when she and her son were not separate, but a single body. A time when he'd been a seed sprouting inside her, planted by the wild, tumultuous need of my parents' young love. Her own blood had coursed through his body, nourishing him through the cord that connected them. At that moment I sensed she'd relinquish her own lifeblood to save that of her firstborn.

During the endless—but too short—hours, Mom and Dad held his hands in the numb silence. And then the monitor squealed, cleaving the room in half, and the green line on the monitor fell flat. Their deadpan eyes turned to me, negating the morbid reality that their son was dead. I hugged them hard and buried their denial when I softly said, "He's gone."

Our red eyes watched Ron's body morph from pink to blue in a green room that was loud with no white noise and no more second chances to say *I love you.*

Today, I hug my grown children when I greet them and again when I reluctantly let them go to continue their busy lives. And when they come to be with me during my final hours, they will know what to do. We've had "the talk," the end-of-life discussion. They will know to hug me. They will know to stroke my arms and tell me that everything will be okay.

Poetry/Mary Schmidt

A Glow in the Night

In a tent of blankets past bedtime hours
she peers at pages flashed by light
dancing through meadows of storylines and flowers
pages touched by the roots, she turns each one.

She enters words of creativity
becomes rich with understanding
savors each phrase like a wild strawberry
consumes each colorful narration.

Closing the door in real life time
I recall reading similar adventures
grateful her learning past the hour of nine
prefers parchment over the glow of television plasma.

Poetry/Frances Ann Crowley

Imminence

Yesterday, a whiff of autumn brought on a surge
of desperate recreation—one last pontoon ride,
one final good buy at the flea, one more s'more.

Meanwhile, aspen trees shivered and chattered,
moms and kids hit the big box store, and
the owl cried, "Too soon, too soon."

Today, swarms of Asian lady beetles and
zucchini have landed on your porch.
You wring your hands and wonder what to do,
while the kitchen clock drips on
and that old fiddler of the cricket clan
chafes away in the ashes of the fire pit.

Leaves, footloose, line dance across your sidewalk,
then tango and rumba all over each other
in the rush to go back.

You help yourself to the last of the refrigerator pickles,
make a pie with the ripest peaches,
and stare out the kitchen window at bits of
age-spotted skin still clinging to the bones of birches.

Poetry/Nancy Devine

Fifth Crow Wing Lake

We ride low in the water, nearly water ourselves,
a Rock-Em-Sock-Robot head named Evinrude
bolted to our canoe's silver collar,
front end an amped up Brahma bull,
back end lake lowrider at the beginning of another July.
Sunday night. Back at our cabin, a load of soggy
washing waiting to dry.

Starboard, a man in jeans and T-shirt casts from his aluminum
       dock
toward a grid of metal and sky shine reflected
above sunnies and walleyes;
the spray on my face is nothing at all like any tears.

If I could look down on us, I'd see us
in portrait layout on God's print preview.

Who knew we were this beautiful?

Poetry/Ruth M. Schmidt-Baeumler

Waiting for the Baby

Summer squeezes drops of water out of thirsty crops.
Onion leaves wilt, potatoes unable to flower stagnate.
Sprinklers set on mechanical trolleys stutter repeats of jets
displaying rainbows just above the ground.

The baby sloshes in embryonic fluids unaware of drought.
It is biding time with cell expansion clocked by stretch-mark
rivulets circling the mother's out-turned navel.

Waiting-for-baby afternoons flicker by with a cake baker in
        Hoboken,
an emergency ward in London, and a Mexican dog
        whisperer in L. A.,
a daily sameness interrupted only by Norwegian TV
        commercials.

This baby mirrors its own mother's birth thirty-eight years
        earlier.
The baby is overdue, it is sweltering hot, it is in a foreign
        country.
But this time the new mother's mother is on hand.

Finally they drag out the tattered deck of UNO.
Memories of family vacations and inside jokes turn up with
        the cards.
The Norwegian spouse doesn't get it but is happy
her mate is distracted. The baby learns trampoline tricks
as the diaphragm jiggles with laughter.

> > >

The baby bulge does not fit behind the car's steering wheel.
The to-be grandma drives the encapsulated couple along
      narrow gravel roads
to shops and the doctor. Four Saturday mornings local
      musicians,
whose stage backdrop is a shimmering lake, help whittle
      away time
as they wait for the baby.

A last pitch plea not be born on its mother's birthday thrums
      its way
through layers of skin, muscle, and fat to baby's aqueous
      harbor.
The baby respects its mother's wishes and one day before,
Emil slips out of the irrigated den creating his singular
day, hour, minute, and sun sign.

Creative Nonfiction/*Reprinted from *Talking Stick 14, 2005/*
Beth Diane Bradley (previously published under Beth Bradley Walter)

There's Nothing Like the Real Thing, Baby

Shortly before my thirtieth birthday, I finally achieved my long-awaited goal of becoming a mother. In preparation, I read several child-development books, went to prenatal classes and followed all the advice of the day bestowed upon pregnant women. In other words, I was ripe for motherhood.

Although planning a pregnancy when you are ready for the responsibility of a child is ideal, it is not everyone's reality. And that is the reason why educators conceived the simulated experience sometimes referred to as "Baby Think it Over." This pint-sized mechanical bull is supposed to show teens how much work and responsibility there is in caring for an infant. The faux baby cries when she is hungry, wet, cold or handled improperly. In theory, the experience should convince them to postpone parenthood until they are adults.

My seventeen-year-old came home one day and announced he was going to be "Dad" of the class baby for the next forty-eight hours. I was curious how he would approach his temporary fatherhood—would he hear the baby crying over his heavy metal music blaring from the basement? And since he hadn't yet mastered the art of hanging up a wet towel without a reminder, how would he deal with a wet diaper?

My questions were soon answered, as little Kelsey Lynn—named after his two best girlfriends—arrived right on schedule, unlike any real baby I've ever known. My son explained she had a mechanism inside that recorded everything that happens to her. He wouldn't let me hold her in case I did it wrong, because it might register as Shaken Baby Syndrome. I recalled how careful I was with my own babies, but respected his concern and kept my hands off of my short-term "grandchild."

To be honest, it wasn't that hard to leave her alone, because she wasn't real enough to be tempting. I noticed the dog was in agreement, because every time the baby cried, he would cock his head, trying to figure out what this strange-smelling, noisy creature was all about. But even he had no interest in getting up close and personal.

I smiled at the sight of my son sitting at the computer—baby cradled in one arm, typing his over-due term paper with the other hand. Multi-tasking, I thought—definitely a necessary parenting skill. He even had to line up a babysitter so he could go to work at his part-time job.

After a long day of being a dad, he was rewarded with more sleep than most new parents get in the first three months. The little robo-tyke only demanded to be fed once during the night.

When I got home the next day, he announced he got an A on the baby project. Although I was very proud of him, I wasn't sure it had served its purpose—because he said he actually missed little Kelsey Lynn.

Back to the drawing board for "Baby Think It Over."

Maybe the experience should start with a pill that causes fake labor pains. After all, even real dads claim to experience psychosomatic symptoms when their wives are pregnant.

And the baby should be programmed to stay awake all night long and have a little colic. Make that a lot of colic—the kind that causes parents to take their babies for a drive to a foreign country, hoping to finally lull them to sleep.

It wouldn't hurt if she spit up all over the car for a grand finale. Right before senior prom, eliminating the need for one of those little pine-scented air fresheners to impress his date. Because when it comes to the smell of spit-up, you can run but you can't hide.

When he becomes a parent for real, I bet he'll change his mind and let Grandma hold the baby once in a while. If he looks in the mirror, he'll notice he hardly has any dents in his head.

After all, free babysitting just might come in handy.

Poetry/Kit Rohrbach

Cleaning the Attic

forty-year-old baby clothes

college blue books,
both mine and the baby's

a milk glass chicken
homeless
since her nesting bowl got
            broken

a tablecloth crocheted
to fit a table
I no longer own, and lately
a nesting place for mice

a child's sled (mine)
hockey trophies (not mine)
Atlantic City souvenirs
reminiscent of salt water
and taffy

income tax forms
from years I've forgotten

collected in a file box
the key is lost

a manual typewriter with
old words tangled
in its red and black ribbon

books I've been meaning to
            donate
but might want to read again
someday

doors I've taken down
because I don't like doors
especially locked ones

except the door to the attic
closed and locked behind me
as I head back downstairs
a dusty copy of *Black Beauty*
tucked under my arm

Poetry/Richard Fenton Sederstrom

Momentary Seas

Not breakers. Our boat is only jostled,
      rolls in decaying waves from
            the ski-boat plowing a straight
      path after the violence
of its heavy-leaning turn,
      the idle and clumsy maneuver
            that spilled its innocent skier.
      The white-capped waves
tumble off to the west of us.

A heavy ski-boat,
      probably water-ballasted
            to heave more of the lake
      out toward the lure
it dragged behind, before the lure,
      the bait, the sacrificial sunburn,
            gave way to centrifugal force
      and its appetite for sport
and more sport and no end of sport.

Gas-guzzling, wasteful and laden
      with suburban hubris we suppose.
            But the accident of wake! awakening
      minutes of majesty left behind,
the kind and generous sweep of seas!
      We are left here rocking and ignored
            to discover alone the passing
      dignity of its white-capped
wash and heave of blue.

Poetry/*Honorable Mention*/Deb Schlueter

Pregnancy

You trudge up the hill, dragging a sled behind you, your footsteps visible in the well-trampled snow. Breath fogging in the February air, you reach the top as the sun sets. With nowhere to go but back down, you settle onto the sled and push off. At first the sled goes slowly. It's not too fast—nothing you can't handle. But as the stars glimmer to life overhead, you hit a patch of ice and skid out of control. You want to stick out your feet and scream for it to stop, that it's going too fast, that you're not ready . . . but you can't. It's too late; your destination is inevitable. Hidden in the dark ahead of you, seconds or minutes away, is the bottom of the hill and the jump you know is there. With no other choice, you curl your fingers around the edge of the fast-moving sled, squeeze your eyes shut, and pray that you manage to stick the landing.

Poetry/Marlys Guimaraes

Sunday Best

I remove dirt-crusted boots,
throw off jeans, soil-hardened,
discard a shirt, stained at the belly.

Grime swirls the shower drain as
my skin sweetens when lathered
with the flowers of Dove soap.

The scrub brush burns. It
eliminates embedded maps of dirt
on scoured knees and elbows.

When my best dress of black silk
slips over my head to glide down my body,
I savor the smell of fresh laundry,

then step into red strappy sandals.
My makeup is minimal. I refuse to compete
with the brilliance of moss roses and

the dazzle of orange daylilies.
The blooming tea roses and fresh cut grass
eliminate the need for perfume at pulse points.

When the teapot whistles, I am reminded
to prepare my favorite tea—Mango Green.
I descend the deck steps, carrying the teacup

as if it were a bridal bouquet, sit in an Adirondack
chair resting on the rise overlooking the garden.
I nod to the statue of St. Fiacre, the Patron Saint of

Gardens, positioned under the trellis
of scarlet-blooming runner beans.
Phoebes and chickadees sing hymns
and together we rejoice.

Buoyancy

"This fishing thing's not all it's cracked up to be," my mother says. Waves gently slap the side of the boat as my pole bends up and down. We've been together for five days straight, trolling for the elusive walleye for hours. "The lakes are so much cleaner up here. It must be the long winters that keep it so pristine," she says. "The cold keeps the riff-raff out; it keeps the crime rates down."

We are drifting towards the other side of the lake and a family of loons floats by: a mother, a father and two brown babies. There's something beautiful yet sad about this happy little family, about the transitory nature of things. One of the adults bends its neck and then disappears beneath the surface.

"You take this fishing thing entirely too seriously," she says. "I might as well be out here talking to myself."

I reel in my line and check my bait. "You're the one who said you're tired of catching sunfish. I'm just trying to catch us a big one."

My mother lights up a cigarette. I grab a handful of sunflower seeds from the bag. I notice my scratched-up hands, which have been cut by the sharp fins of fish who've tried to wriggle free from my grip all week. There's black dirt underneath my nails (probably from the worm bait). I toss the seeds into my mouth anyway.

"Why'd we decide to do this? We could be getting mother-daughter massages and manicures instead of threading hooks with worms and leeches." She chuckles.

We both know neither one of us is the spa type. All that pampering seems fake. Give me the real and the visceral, the struggle and the fight. Give me the cleaning of the fish: the scraping of scales from skin, the filleting of the flesh, the tossing of the bones, the guts and then let me deep-fry that meat, chew it up and swallow it.

I spit a mouthful of cracked-open shells into the water and watch them float away.

"Get the net, get the net," she yells.

My mother is leaning over the side of the boat, reeling in her line excitedly. As she gets her catch closer to the boat she mumbles, "Damn weeds." Sure enough, her hook is covered in a wad of green slime, but underneath is a tiny wiggling perch. We giggle as I unhook him and toss him back into the water.

The wind has died down. The lake is calm and serene. In the distance we hear the calling of loons. "It's such an eerie sound isn't it?" she asks. "Did you know they have different calls for different things they're trying to tell each other?"

"Yes," I answer. "I think they are telling each other, 'I am here, I am here.'"

There's something shadowy and shifty about loons. It's as if they have the power to call forth all we have ignored. I am thinking about the distant call of the Sirens, those dangerous and beautiful mythological creatures who lured sailors into crashing into the rocky shore.

"You're not very good with that trolling motor," she says. "We're zig-zagging all over."

"I wish the grandkids were here," she says. "It would have been more fun."

We had already discussed this. I had booked this far enough in advance and told my three nearly grown kids to be here but it didn't work out. But she's not talking about my kids; she means my sister's sons, Dylan and Benny, who have both died.

I notice her gaze. On the shore an elderly man is chasing around a little boy and they are both laughing. Is she thinking of them? I do not ask. This is a sorrow I cannot fix. This is a sadness I cannot catch. *Don't pick up her grief. This is what it is like to be alone on a boat with your mother who has endured so many losses*, I tell myself.

It is nearly sunset. The cabins are lit up with an easy-going yellow light where large families sit at tables. Laughter permeates through open windows, bonfires abound and the smell of burning wood brings back memories. I ask, "Remember that camping trip when Dylan ate a minnow? Was that the same year he tipped me over in the canoe?"

She doesn't answer, but the loons continue to whine, *I am here, I am here.*

Those families used to be us. I want it all back for her: husband, grandkids, a retirement package they advertise on TV. She is looking her age and I start to wonder how many more memories I will make with her.

And now my mood has shifted from peaceful oblivion to despondency: God of water, God of mothers, God of widows, God of grandmothers, God of dead grandbabies, God of Nothing and God of Everything, God of this terrible beauty of existence, God of lakes and these long-winded loons, we are here, we are over frickin' here!

More silence. We are barely drifting. The battery's nearly dead on the trolling motor. Finally I say, "Unlike this boat, nothing can truly carry us through life."

She exhales. I get a whiff of second-hand smoke as she says, "Sometimes I really worry about you."

"You worry about *me*?" I ask, surprised.

My mother—mother of three daughters, whose maternal assignment has never been easy—she's got one daughter grieving the loss of her children and another with a traumatic brain injury. I'm the lucky one. It's never occurred to me that she'd worry about me.

"Well, of course. You're always diving into the deep end. I wish you'd lighten up and enjoy life a little more," she says.

I stare at her in astonishment. My mother: nearly seventy years old with hunched over shoulders, wearing a crooked grin, a tie-dyed T-shirt, and a baseball cap that says PADDLE FASTER, I HEAR BANJO MUSIC.

"And you know what else?" She asks, "You know that saying about how life's a hundred percent attitude? Well, that's a load of crap. Half of it's luck. Just think, we could've been born into the Taliban. We sure wouldn't be out here enjoying this sunset."

"That's very true." I chuckle, nodding my head.

My mother: always trying like hell to be an optimist, still offering up encouragement like she did when I was a kid. Maybe I've had it all wrong this whole time we've been fishing. Instead of me being worried I'd pick up her grief, maybe she's just trying to not pick up mine.

"I'm sick of fishing," she says. "Let's go watch CSI."

Poetry/Joel Van Valin

Wind and Trees

The spring water
was chill to the skin
so we found some trees
to take shelter in.

The rain ran out;
the wind came rough.
The trees showered on us
what they had kept off.

We walked under a sky
now stripped bare to the stars—
free from the wind and trees
and their little wars.

Poetry/Sharon Harris

Krista Joy

that would have been her name
this daughter I never had
the name is one I always loved
both crisp and joyous on my tongue

I met her once in a dream
more real than most days
I spent a long night rolling in the covers
dreaming I was in labor
dreaming I was bringing her
into the world

I don't know now how old I was then
or who I was with—was I married or single?
it didn't matter
only she mattered

I know I held her in my arms
for a time in this dream
and gazed into her face
I remember the warmth of her—
the overwhelming swell of protectiveness
that rose up in my heart—

and I remember
the speechless grief I felt
when I woke
to find her gone

Poetry/Tim J. Brennan

On a Streetcar in San Francisco

A young woman looks at me
with penny-sized eyes.
In the half-light she could be the first
girl I ever kissed.
She smells of ocean kelp,
undulating waves or sand
and empty shells.

I try to ignore her, ashamed
of her pain so real I could reach
out and touch it.

She smiles and stumbles
to the next car, clutching
against a steel bar for balance,
a knot of arms and desperation
in the traveling glass.

She might fit inside me
but I won't let her.

Creative Nonfiction/Marlene Mattila Stoehr

For I was Hungry. . .

By that evening the waitress had fallen into the habit of merely pointing us to our usual booth. Our hotel was across the street and, after exhausting hours exploring what the big city and attractions reachable on one-day tours had to offer, we usually had only enough energy to say, "Let's eat at the Chinese place again."

Our booth was the one closest to the entrance, where I had an unobstructed view of the entire dining room while my husband could watch patrons coming or leaving. I ordered sweet and sour chicken served with a vegetable-laden rice. As before, I noted that the servings were far too generous for one person to consume comfortably.

Two women in the next booth were immersed in an animated and prolonged conversation. I wondered about their relationship, perhaps mother-daughter, perhaps aunt-niece.

Meanwhile a man, forty years old or so, came into the restaurant. Immediately a woman bartender came from the adjacent lounge area and indicated that he could not come in there. He stood a moment, then, somewhat unsteadily, made his way to a booth across from us and sat down. The server brought him a glass of ice water and a menu that he glanced over briefly, then put down on the seat beside him.

I studied him briefly and wondered about his circumstances. Long hair spilled out from under a cap pulled low over his forehead. His brown jacket remained zipped tight over his slight body. Bright yellow laces on his scuffed shoes might have been the newest item in his wardrobe.

Although I would guess he was homeless—the city has many homeless people—he did not appear to be dirty. Perhaps he could best be described as appearing hopeless. He sat motionless without looking around, merely sat, as if waiting. The waitress did not approach him to take an order.

By now the women in the next booth had finished eating and the older one asked for a take-out box that she filled with her leftover rice. She put that container in a plastic bag and tied it carefully with a secure knot to make it easy to carry.

Perhaps she noticed the man for the first time as she paid their bill at the cash register. At the point I next saw her, she had walked over to him and handed him her take-out box, saying simply, "God bless you." He nodded a response and put the box on the table without opening it.

I had eaten all of my meal that I cared for, so when the waitress offered me a take-out box I impulsively asked, "Could I give the rest of this to that man?"

She double-checked my intent. With a slight motion of her head, she stated, "You want to give this to him." I nodded. She picked up my used fork and my plate with the uneaten sweet and sour chicken with rice, carried it over and placed it in front of him. Without looking around, without a word, he began to dine. At one point he opened and added the container of gifted rice to his plate, squashing down the square mound of cold rice with both hands, and continued to eat.

Then, as silently as he had eaten, the man left the restaurant and returned to the streets.

Poetry/Meridel Kahl

Oilcloth

We enter a café near the canal.
Before we sit—
as if on cue
as if in prayer
with breath held—
we rub our palms in slow circles
across the oilcloth tabletop.

Fragments of memory,
ordinary things
from another time—

egg coffee in
a big enamel pot
wood-handled forks
with three tines
a dry sink
a bucket of cool water—

awaken from deep sleep
and stretch into the room
as our hands linger
on glossy clouds of pink peonies
in fields of bright blue.

Poetry/Cheryl Weibye Wilke

Not Yet

Sometimes I look at you when you're not
looking at me . . . in your bed sleeping, at the counter
studying, in the car jiving to your tunes . . . and I see

time passing by. You are inching up. Won't be long
and you'll be taller than me. Your feet
longer than what's left of the road

I'm traveling. Daughter,

for now, let's sing to this journey together. Me
at the wheel. You at the dial. Circles. Rings. 'Round
and around. Let's ride these flying horses

on into tomorrow.

Creative Nonfiction/Deb Schlueter

Minnesota Shade

An ancient red oak guarded our Brainerd Lakes backyard for more than a century. Its huge leaves protected a colony of squirrels and its acorns littered the ground every autumn. Our dogs picked its spreading shade as a favorite nap spot—perfect for watching for trespassing critters. The tree stood tall and proud in the background of many family pictures.

A July storm brought it crashing down. My husband and I counted ourselves lucky. Thousands of trees had been lost in that storm; at least none of ours had ended up on the house.

We planned to mourn its passing in practical, Minnesota fashion—a funeral dirge played on chainsaws, an old tractor for a hearse, cremation in our wood stove as its final goodbye. This came to a halt when I saw the beautiful grain of its wood, littered with the marks of bugs and time and the past, the history of our land written inside the tree.

A treasure like this couldn't just be turned into firewood. There had to be something better, although I had no idea what it could be.

For weeks the tree lay in the yard as my husband contemplated the possibilities. Then, with the roar of a chainsaw, he turned the tree into eight-foot lengths and dragged them up the hill. He ran the logs through a handmade lumber mill to create thick, wide boards and carted those into the woodshed to dry. I asked several times what he had planned, but he only smiled.

Summer turned to autumn, then to winter, and the quiet January days brought time to work on the old tree. My husband toted the boards from the shed to the garage to be carefully planed and sanded. He scrutinized the wood for allure and charm, and picked out the best boards. Over the course of two weeks, he glued them together into a large slab, perfecting the smooth surface with epoxy to fill in the holes and knots, and I started to guess what he was building.

One day I walked into the garage to find a rustic-style kitchen table. Easily four feet wide and nine feet long, the thing was massive. With a little more sanding and a few coats of varnish to protect the wood, my husband finally proclaimed it finished.

The table now dominates our dining room. My dogs have found its shadowed recesses a great place to nap during bright afternoons. Its glossy surface reflects the view through the windows. With eight chairs arranged around its rough-hewn edges, it stands ready for crowds of family to descend upon it this summer.

Less than a hundred feet from where it spent its life growing, our old oak tree will stay a part of our family pictures. A century of life is etched into its patterns and swirls. Perhaps, several generations from now, someone will sit at the table and be able to read the history of our own lives in the scratches and nicks it has yet to earn.

Poetry/ *Reprinted from Talking Stick 10, 2001/*
Florence Witkop

Dragon Fire

It's common knowledge, everybody knows,
That unicorns were horses long ago,
Convergently evolving like albino rhinos
Till attaining perfect symbiosis
With virgin woodland nymphs.
It's common knowledge, everybody knows.

It's equally well known how rabbits have evolved:
Though multicolored camouflage is evolutionarily extreme
Against the limpid green of spring,
Considering how rabbits multiply,
Sheer numbers indicate that Easter-egg-to-rabbit
Is one of nature's more successful schemes.
It's common knowledge, everybody knows.

But less well known or understood,
With questions far exceeding firmly stated facts,
Is where and when and how and why
Dragons and dinosaurs diverged
And which breathed fire first and flew upon pearlescent wings,
And which died first millennia ago
Till all were gone.

Or did they merely duplicate stealth mode
And even now glide
Silently . . .
Invisibly . . .
Through brightly colored autumn leaves
On many-splendored membrane wings
At sunset, breathing dragon fire?

Poetry/Sue Reed Crouse

Love Like That

Some time has passed since your beloved died in your arms,
clouded eyes never closing so you could be the last sight.

Your friends say, *Move on, find a new love.*
Never again, you say. *Love like that comes once in a lifetime.*
They reply that *love like that* is precisely why you need another
   beloved.

There is an impasse.

One day, you meet a being so beautiful,
that all your cells align their electric charges.
Cloud to cloud lightning, and *never*
flies away in one joyous shake.

Your new beloved does not replace the old.
You simply grow a new heart alongside the broken one.

You swing in the hammock together, limbs entwined.
Side by side, you crouch by the pond, examining frogs.
You sleep in the curve of one another, bodies sharing warmth.

Your old beloved and your new, your broken heart
and your bursting one, wrap their roots around one another.

Time passes like a string of the sweetest summers.

One day, your new beloved relaxes, like your last,
into your arms. Eyes open, final sigh, absolutely no fear,

offering a final gift—
small wag of a stubby tail.

Fiction/*Editor's Choice*/Tarah L. Wolff

When I Fell for Him

"Let's go to the railroad bridge."

"What about the red one?"

(It was a fair inquiry; the red one was the one this town was known for. On every calendar and ad that proclaimed that this was a tourist destination was that damned red bridge.)

I said, "You can see it from there."

What was I going to tell my niece about the old railroad bridge?

I said, "A kid died last summer jumping off it."

"That's awful! How stupid are people?"

"Yeah, right?" I faked a laugh. "No kidding!"

There were signs everywhere, begging kids not to jump and proclaiming that it was illegal. Apparently no one told that kid to jump right in the middle because I knew if he had jumped in the middle, he would have been safe. The bridge arched over twenty feet above the river.

It smelled like lake water. Like literal Minnesota. Old folks were feeding the ducks by the DO NOT JUMP signs. They were flapping and nibbling (as ducks do). We walked right out to the very center and I leaned in the middle on the smooth steel railing. She leaned with me and we looked out over the green water.

*

He had not taken my hand ("friends" were watching). We hauled ourselves up; he didn't dare give me a boost in front of anyone. The "friends" who had wanted to do this (indeed, who had TALKED us into this) stood back and watched, no doubt ready to flee at the first sign of trouble.

We got up and stood side by side.

I could hear his breath. I swore I could feel the heat coming off him. His heart was racing. So was mine. My pants and coat were on the bridge behind me and it was cold. Goose bumps swept over me like blankets of winter.

We were going to do it.

The steel was freezing under my bare feet. We didn't look at each other but our hearts were beating madly, in tandem. We were too close for jumping this far up. Our arms brushed but neither of us adjusted; it was the first time we got to really touch. It was black out and the streetlights gave us nothing but a glimmer of waves a hundred miles below.

"You ready?" I was out of breath.

He just laughed.

Of course he was.

Was I?

I laughed because I could do nothing else.

I'd made this jump before when I was a kid; what made this time so special?

I started the countdown through my chattering teeth.

He joined me on "Two."

*

She said, "This is beautiful!"

She was looking at the park up the river and the red arching bridge with its quaint wooden rails. I nodded in agreement. I was smiling. It was summer and everything made sense in the summer in Minnesota. There were things to do and everything was easier.

She said, "This is really neat! When did they put this up?"

I shrugged. "Years ago. That restaurant over there sits where the railroad depot used to be. That's why it's called The Boxcar."

"Really?"

"I have no idea. But it makes sense. Right?"

She laughed and shook her head at me, leaning over the railing. "I would totally jump!"

I just laughed at her and shook my head, feigning that I didn't agree with her at all.

*

We hit "One." The countdown was over. Every part of me was shaking; adrenaline raced through me like liquid steel.

I jumped, wondering if he would.

Of course he did.

The rush was warmer than the air and I waited. It was like hanging somewhere after time had stopped. I could hear nothing but the wind; my heart was gone, my cold skin was gone, left somewhere above me where gravity remained.

I wondered if I would ever hit.

We jumped too close.

Legs and bodies smacked into the water and plunged down. A slap of defiant wet. A rebel scream into the cold fall night. Haul us away but first we will jump!

It was fucking cold and I didn't care that my neck and collarbone hurt like hell. We had jumped and come up. We did not fall forever. He took my hand after the doggy paddle to the shore and it felt so good and warm. He rushed to help me up now, to touch me; no one was watching, so he could. It was black and the rocks were slippery as we stumbled to shore.

We got up and came up well apart. Nothing to do with each other.

Our "friends" were bored and acting like they had walked over here just so we could jump and they had grown very tired of doing what "we" wanted to do. (Never mind it was them who had talked us into it.)

No one helped me get dressed but I eventually got my skinny jeans on over my soaked, freezing body. We walked away to go find more alcohol, he and I staying a far safer distance apart now. But I was vastly aware of my body's awareness of him and I knew our hearts were still beating together.

*

I pushed myself off the rail. "Let's go see the red bridge."

She said, "I like this one. This one feels good and old. I know why someone would want to jump off of it."

"Oh, yeah?"

She said, "It feels safe."

I laughed. "As long as you jump in the middle and not too close to anybody!"

"Have you jumped off it?" she gasped accusingly as we sashayed to the other side.

I couldn't help myself and smoothed my gray hair back and pulled my shirt away so she could see the scar on my collarbone.

"Holy shit, what did you hit?"

"Your uncle Ted! It's perfectly safe. You just gotta jump far enough apart!"

I pointed us toward the red bridge as she dissolved in a laughing fit.

"No one jumps here anymore," I said.

"Not that little boy apparently . . ."

"Oh, he knew. I think they would have a better chance of keeping kids from jumping if they took all the signs down."

Everyone had said that he had been goaded into it but no one could prove that the boy had not been alone. I guess we all learn that some "friends" are like that. I guess it made no difference to the boy as he would swim for eternity and part of me wondered how wrong that could be. Would that not be my hope for the end? The rush of lake water hitting me so hard that everything evaporates? What if we could run around and keep doing that forever?

I looked back at the bridge. What if he still was?

Slipping on lake rocks in the middle of August, by the time he reached the center he was hot enough to want to go again. Scramble, scramble, pull, pull. Get himself up there. Right in the middle now because nothing else matters except to hit and sink as deep as possible.

But I do wonder if, even in eternity, for a split second before he hits, if he wonders like I did, if he will ever hit or if he will just keep falling forever.

Everybody knows the fall is the best part.

Poetry/Jeanne Emrich

Hiding Places

Like wintering swans, together
we learn where the open water is, together
we hide in plain sight at ice's edge.
Then the sun sets and we tuck ourselves away,
each into our own feathery depths. We float
as islands in separate dreams. But I would like
to say we are never really apart. I keep nothing
from you and you, me, that even in our dreams,
we can read each other's unblinking face
and know our individual truths as one,
our radiant, shared nows, our hiding places
within each other.

Poetry/Kathryn Knudson

As Long As the Wish

I fell back, arms outstretched,
hit the snow shrieking. My legs
scissored in-and-out. Arms slid

purposefully. I laughed toward
the sky. And then, too quickly, my
enjoyment was over. Every time.

The cold always leached in and
sliced to skin, usually at my ankles
where I'd outgrown the snowpants

my parents would have replaced
had the drought not lasted another
summer. And of course I couldn't

get up without ruining the effect,
thanks to an errant elbow or indent
from a hip. Snow angels never looked

as good as I thought they should. As
good as I wished they would. But still
I tipped back again and again. Creating

a choir. Building an army. Every fall
was a rush of exhilaration, a flare of
fear without any real danger from the

cushion of snow, a moment without
worry about everything I knew I
couldn't change. Every time I raised

my arms and let go, being a kid, being
me, felt perfect, a feeling that was as
short as an instant, as long as the wish.

Poetry/Miriam Weinstein

Today—This Poem We're Writing Together

A derailment in Wisconsin—18,000 gallons
of ethanol spilled in the Mississippi. In the distance
bald eagles soaring, plunging into this bulge in the river
called Lake Pepin.

Gasoline. How we love it.

Ethanol. Crude oil. Crossing our country on rails built
for old freight trains. Winding past farms. Fields.
Whistle-stop towns. Cutting through the heart
of our cities.

Later—another derailment—another spill.
Crude oil in a different river. *Nothing more than an accident*
the investigators say, shaking their heads, lowering their eyes
as if in prayer.

Poetry/Peggy Trojan

The Harness Bells

Four silver bells
on the ten-inch piece
of cracked old leather
Mother saved
from the homestead
can whisk me back in time
more than a hundred years
Shake in sync
with the trot of horses
and I become my mother
tucked between her parents
in the sleigh
Frankie and Dickie
know the way home
nostrils blowing steam
in the cold night full of stars
Bundled in quilts and happiness
believing the whole world
is at peace

Poetry/Linda Maki

Cross Body

It dangled from a wire hanger, one side
drooped lower than the other. The last thing
I had bought her when frail arms quivered
with the weight of her everyday carryall.
Look Mom, how lightweight, it's a cross body.

Zippered by strangers into a black plastic bag
and wheeled into the hall. I grabbed the purse
from the bedside table. Slung just once onto bony
shoulders, weakened by chemo needles, absent appetite.
Grief tucked it safely in the back of my closet.

Five years later I part waves of clothing,
pull suitcases from dark corners, toss
shoes into piles. Reach, grasp, inhale.
Inside a Kleenex nestled with two sticks
of Juicy Fruit. Her last will and testament.

Poetry/Jeanne A. Everhart

Women Without Husbands

We had them once
loved them
they were taken from us
suddenly
not by other women
but that dark spectre
we didn't see lurking

We are women without husbands
not single women
for we still feel
married to our lost love
I cannot utter Widow
that old woman's name
is not mine

We are women without husbands
gathering Sundays after church
at the local restaurant for lunch
knowing the feeling
of helpmates searching
to mend that tear in our hearts
with companionship

Fiction/Candace Simar

Out of Sync

Oscar and Ruby Ryerson moved to the old schoolhouse after their farmhouse burned down last year. Oscar lost a foot to sugar diabetes about the same time, and their kids carried on fit to be tied about them moving into the old folks' home in Wild Rose.

Oscar refused to budge. "I've lived in this township all my life, and I'll die here," he said. That was that. Oscar usually got his way.

The schoolhouse was one room with windows on all sides. It was too small, and he was always under Ruby's feet, but at least it wasn't the rest home. Oscar admired the symmetry of identical porches gracing two sides—better than the lopsided woodshed tacked onto the old farmhouse. Oscar liked things orderly and harmonious. A perfectionist, his daughters said.

Oscar figured his life was about over, anyway. Once he kicked the bucket, Ruby could move into town with the girls, and live it up on the insurance money. That's the way of it. The man worked himself into the crapper, and the wife reaped the rewards.

Ruby was at her wits' end. Oscar took no interest in anything. He wouldn't watch TV, and turned the radio off as fast as she turned it on. He claimed the Minnesota Twins had broken his heart, and the Vikings beyond hopeless. "I can look outside and see for myself," he said one day when Ruby wanted to leave the weather channel going. "Don't need some New York city slicker to tell me it's raining."

Oscar avoided the front porch because it gave a clear view of the power lines that stretched to Williston and beyond. He named them monsters, strange humming beasts that, like him, rooted to the ground on one foot and waited for the end. Ruby called him a crazy old coot. Then she telephoned their daughters for advice. They all agreed he was losing his mind.

On the back stoop, Oscar saw only waving grass, meadowlarks, sometimes a jack rabbit or coyote slipping by. He resisted the temptation of taking his gun for a final walk out onto the prairie. It would be over fast and easy. He thought about it every day, but couldn't do it to Ruby, not after all their years together. Besides, Judgment Day loomed. He had enough on his plate without adding a mortal sin.

Ruby did her best. The doctor said sugar diabetes would be his death if he didn't quit the sweets. Ruby hid the cookie jar, but Oscar found it every time. She couldn't understand why his blood sugar skyrocketed even after she banished sweets from the house, until she found Oscar's stash of candy bars in the trunk of their car.

"Good God, no," Oscar said one day when a huge truck pulled up to the house. "They're building more power lines!" He tottered on crutches over to the work crew.

"Nope," the foreman said. "Wind turbines."

All his life, Oscar had battled prairie winds. Winds parched the corn in drought, wilted the beans in the heat of summer and froze his blood during the frigid North Dakota winters. Oscar couldn't count how many hats it had taken, good ones worth real money. Folks on the prairie learned to live with it or moved on, somewhere beyond the tree lines where they could find shelter from its never-ending howl.

To think those same winds could light cities, be useful for something other than misery, made him ponder the mysteries of the universe. And he, Oscar Ryerson, stood witness to the greatest advancement of wind energy the country had seen.

He hurried back into the house, stabbing the crutches into the prairie grass and swinging his good foot forward.

"Ruby!" he yelled.

Ruby came running, wiping her hands on her apron and expecting the worst. Instead he babbled about turbines, progress and harnessing prairie winds.

"Get me to the *liberry*," he said. "I got to study up."

Ruby fussed with her wispy hair, and backed the Tempest

out of the shed. She couldn't remember the last time Oscar had shown interest in something new. The library at Wild Rose filled only a small corner in the hardware store, but Oscar found a *Time Warner* book on wind power.

Every day he sat on the back stoop paging through the book, as the work crew laid the footings for fifty wind turbines. When the book came due at the library, Oscar made an astounding statement.

"Call and order up a copy. It's only $89.99."

Ruby's hands trembled as she dialed the toll free number. Then she sneaked the cordless phone into the bathroom, and called her daughter in Williston. That wind farm was the best thing that ever happened, they both agreed.

Oscar attended a "Q and A" session at the town hall. When a redneck from Ross raised conspiracy theories, Oscar slowly pulled himself to his good foot.

"It's only sensible," Oscar said in a matter-of-fact voice. "No one wants dependence on Middle Eastern oil." Later Ruby told their daughter that he sounded wise as a judge and glib as a Philadelphia lawyer.

Oscar scribbled letters to the editor, dialed call-in programs on the radio and watched the workmen haul massive parts shipped all the way from Germany.

"It's like having my old Oscar back," Ruby told her girls. She dug out the binoculars, and encouraged him to jot notes in a little notebook she bought at the dollar store.

The day the first turbine raised in the periwinkle sky became a day of celebration. Ruby baked a diabetic cake. Oscar felt optimism as he had not known since the early days when everything seemed possible.

The giant white blades turned like a giant pinwheel. He watched them until it was too dark to see, then got up early to be in place before first light. The pink sunrise reflected off the swirling blades. He took his breakfast on the porch so he wouldn't miss a thing, as the construction crew raised the second turbine.

Oscar watched blades catch the morning breeze. The giant machines like dancers, like perfectly matched Clydesdales in the sky, with the blades going 'round in perfect harmony. But then, the new one faltered, lost speed, and stuttered like a cripple.

Oscar raised up with a gasp of horror. This wasn't how it should be.

He called out, cursed, but the blades acted as they wanted to act. One always faster than the other, even though the same prairie wind propelled them. Every so often a brief moment of synchronicity, but then stumbling disarray.

Oscar pawed through the *Time Warner* book, finding the page of turbines. He hadn't noticed before, but the photograph showed different positions of the blades. He had envisioned a field of wind turbines in perfect unison. Instead he would be staring at chaos.

He had been blindsided. He should have known it was too good to be true.

"Ruby!" he said, then remembered Ruby had taken the car into town for canning jars. The work crew readied to place more turbines, turbines that would make him crazy, that would destroy his good humor and push him over the edge once and for all. He had to do something before it was too late. It was up to him to stop this travesty of justice.

He lurched to his feet, dropping the binoculars, grabbing his hunting rifle and crutching out to the construction site.

"Stop!" he said. "No more."

The men saw him coming, and paused from their work. The foreman stepped forward to greet Oscar, but stepped back when he saw the raised gun.

"Stop," Oscar said. "Enough. Not another turbine . . . "

The headache stopped him, a searing pain that robbed his breath and caused him to drop the gun and sink to his knees in the stubbly grass.

"Are you all right?"

Oscar couldn't speak, couldn't answer. He felt the

blackness closing in, as the foreman hollered for someone to dial 911.

Later, when Ruby and their daughters clustered around his hospital bed, Oscar tried to explain what happened. He couldn't speak. His right hand lay like a slab of meat beside him.

"You've had a stroke," Ruby said, stroking his forehead and wiping his mouth with her hanky. "Don't try to talk," she said. "You need rest."

The girls chatted among themselves about how sad it was for him to get sick before the wind farm was finished. They acted like he was already dead. Oscar mumbled, trying to explain the lack of synchronicity, but the words came out as grunts and groans.

At the nursing home, Ruby insisted on a room facing the wind farm. "It's his only pleasure in life," she said, and the girls murmured their agreement.

Oscar waved his good hand, struggling to speak.

"He's wild about wind turbines," Ruby said. "Place his wheelchair in front of the window whenever he's up. He loves to watch them go around."

•

Poetry/*Honorable Mention*/Mary Christine Kane

The Plain Things

Today I wanted
just a picture of you
with your squat dog
in that bright orange sweater
you crocheted for her
so her little white body
wouldn't get lost
in piles of
Buffalo snow.

I remembered,
it is the plain things
we will long for:

The bowl with the gold-scalloped edges
pastel flowers at bottom
ladled full of soup.
Your purse stocked with gum, crackers,
rosaries.

I wanted just a picture,
you planting tomatoes
in that thin strip of dirt lining your driveway,
moss kerchief fluttering.
You stirring sauce
with the burnt-edged wooden spoon.
You crocheting in the parlor,
curious dog by your feet.
You scurrying to the door
fuzzy slippers scraping linoleum
to welcome us in.

Poetry/Frances Ann Crowley

Horses of Another Color

In one of their early conversations,
she told him how over the moon she feels
whenever she sees a carousel.

It was a rainy evening in November.
They had a table by the window
at Lucky's. The light was dying,
most of the leaves had fallen madly
in love with the ground, and the
carnival caravans had long since
packed up and moved south.

They saw each other off and on after that,
but the subject never came up again,
and she muddled through winter and spring
without the benefits of cotton candy.

Then it was June and on her birthday
he surprised her with a book called
Painted Ponies Rendezvous. It was filled
with glossy photos of once-abandoned
carousels that had been restored.

When she cracked the spine, she swore
there was a perfume sample of popcorn
and she kept hearing the come-hither
melodies of a Wurlitzer.

Poetry/Karen Turner

Art Therapist at The Home

Today it's just the two of us.
I sit beside her wheelchair and paste a bare tree shape onto
       paper
And prattle about painting in October's vibrant leaves.

She reaches for the watercolors.
And heads for the ground beneath the tree
Says she's itching to work the soil.
It's been too long.

So she paints lovingly at the roots,
Mixing and sloshing the blacks,
browns and purples.
 She speaks of mixing sand with loam,
mulch from dead leaves of past years.

No, she's not ready to paint the leaves yet.
"First the raindrops and the sun."
Patient blues and yellows.
Her joyfulness gains momentum.
She tells me that lately, she lives in her dreams.

"Now the leaves," she says.
Her paint strokes begin dancing green on bare limbs.
She reaches, reaches to their tips.
We both smile.

Poetry/Susan Niemela Vollmer

Joan

She said that the most difficult aspect was having
to give up making or dreaming about any long range plans
and simply to deal with life minute by minute
or at the most, day by day

She sat at the table thin-faced and scanty-haired
laughed uproariously with me
at the silliness of spouses
parceled out her belongings with notes to explain her bequests

Submerged in pain and drugs
she was herself for only ten minutes a day
the other hours steered her unwillingly
floundering between the billows of darkness toward the light

Poetry / Kathryn Knudson

Mary Bligh, Eighth Floor

I'd been able to forget
how loud hospitals are.
The unceasing rhythm
of beeps and sighs. Drops

of fluid, puffs of breath,
notes of hope. Fluorescent
lighting seems to amplify
the sound—light almost

painful in its intensity
scalding away shadow
without providing comfort,
leaving no sanctuary for

the eye. Light as harsh
and cold as in late winter
when the sun bleaches the
landscape sepia. A winter

day when snowdrifts on the
lake appear wishfully to be
waves poised before breaking.
A day when cross-country

skis swish by and passing
cars hum in the distance,
joining the jagged panting
of distance runners who

squint willfully against the
horizon. A day when tears
well readily in reaction to
the cold and freeze onto

lashes before sliding down
cheeks to splash onto the
stainless steel railing I'm
leaning against for support.

Creative Nonfiction/Jeanne A. Everhart

Stroke

At first my denying mind could not believe dizziness and numbness were a problem. Doctors surround me, and I think I hear the word *stroke*, as blood pressure cuffs, needles, and questions bombard me. Nurses hover all night and the following day checking vitals. The needle from the IV throbs in my wrist but is only an irritation compared to my spinning brain.

My bed with rails is my world. I decide I will not depend on this bell to ring for a nurse to come to my aid. Unfocused eyes and no center of balance create nausea. My life changed in a moment, but I am alive and trying to overcome paralysis. I'm thankful to be alive, have memories, thought processes and creative skills. My mind inhabits someone else's body and I struggle to get mine back.

My first meal in transitional care is in my room. There I have the privacy to eat my pureed spaghetti and drink thickened liquids. Blueberry muffins are served in a brown cup, a dark blue-black unrecognizable paste, but the flavor is there. Though the texture is deceiving, I can pretend I am eating the real thing with the flavor in my mouth. If I use my imagination, the taste of cinnamon, apples and pie crust all pureed together do taste like apple pie. Tiny bites—one half teaspoon—turn my head to the right shoulder, tuck my chin and swallow, swallow again and again. Wait to be sure my airway is clear, then take another bite. A meal takes concentration and a great deal of time to finish.

The nurses and aides wheel people to the table in my wing, but bring my meals to me. The next morning I still do not feel comfortable leaving my secure space and I eat in my room again, as I retrain my throat to swallow.

The following day, I summon my courage and push my

walker to the table with the others and self-consciously eat my meal as a welcome newcomer. I pick my spot at the table with care for the following meals, so I will not offend anyone by turning my head away to swallow when they are in conversation with me. I listen to stories of medical problems around the table: cancer, knee surgery, infections, and organ failures. We exchange bits of life, where we are from, our ailments and we wonder about those unable to get out of bed and join us at the table. For some, transitional care is terminal, but for others just a brief stop in life's unexpected plans.

Individual diets according to the medical problems are the main topic of conversation. "How come you got that?" "I didn't get what she has." "What did you get?" "Did you get chicken soup?" "I got chicken soup." "Do they expect me to eat this?" "Peaches again, canned peaches with everything!"

The Judge is one of my favorite characters. He can barely get in and out of his wheelchair with assistance. He likes to sit in the recliner in front of the television, where he sleeps through most of the ballgames and the news. He enjoys talking about local politics—and, being a retired judge, knows "inside stories."

At the table Marion has fallen asleep through most of the meal and finally asks for assistance back to bed. The Judge eyes her angel food cake heaped with cherries. He is diabetic and has a small piece of bare cake. The rest of us are relishing our desserts overflowing with sweet cherries. His fork reaches into the cake Marion left. He slips cherries into his mouth, smacks his lips, then looks around the table with a smile. We smile back. His fork draws the dessert in front of him and he pushes his over to replace hers. "Is anyone going to tell?" he asks. We all smile, shake our heads and satisfy our sweet tooth. The nurses catch him and he pays with high blood sugar.

I am witnessing the pain of what age and illness do to those we love. Watching a son with his elderly mother, he becomes irritated and leaves abruptly. I feel sorry for her and him too. She sounded a bit demanding, needing her hair curlers and social security card from home. With terminal cancer in her back, a crushed vertebrae, and pneumonia, she is heavily medicated for pain. She sleeps a lot in the bed next to mine and repeats herself, but has a stubborn determination. She cries when her son leaves and says, "Come back sometime," though he cannot hear her weak voice.

I am impressed by the kindness of staff and their patience. Some are so young, but have compassion this woman's son lacks, when she tells them she just feels like crying. Being dependent on others is not easy and is humbling. She hopes to join her husband of fifty-four years in another nursing home soon.

The resident wing is filled with whiteheads in wheelchairs, who feebly exercise. A singer, who thinks he is Willie Nelson but isn't, visits weekly. Some residents sit passively listening. Others make attempts at applause and some sleep. There are sound minds here, with failing bodies. This is an up-close view of the reality of the finality of life.

Clinging to my walker, I pass the nurses' station ten times and counting. I am told forty-five laps equals one mile. If I can walk one mile with my walker, I will be ready to go home. Today that is my goal. My body does not know how to walk without this metal balance support I push on wheels. As I pass the nurses station the forty-fourth time, they cheer me. A nurse runs in front of my walker with a bubble wand for my victory lap. Soap bubbles float around me and I smile at this major milestone for my stroke-impaired body.

Poetry/*Honorable Mention*/Susan McMillan

Memorial Service

Appropriate words went unsaid.
Monster.
Sonofabitch.

Some of six adult children
wore corporeal scars, but all—
chafed by long-gnawed knots of
     gall
unknowing sympathizers
could not see—

attended
to support their mother,
wreck of a woman,
or to see for themselves
it was over.

Before the service
made peculiar by soft words of
sorrow,
loss,

each crept
cautious to the casket
saw him there unmoving
in his brown polyester suit,
ice-hard eyes closed for good.

At the very last she stood,
his wife of forty years,
strode forth
     unaccompanied
to the corpse.

Sly, so no one saw,
she slipped the gold band
from her left-hand finger,
dropped it into dark space
between his right thigh
and ripples of angel-white
     satin.

Ceremony was brief.
Afterwards, gathering,
they spoke of other things.

Creative Nonfiction/Ryan M. Neely

Street Walkers and Cigarettes

At three o'clock in the morning, the streets of Oakland are deserted. Nighttime denizens congregate under parking lot lights of twenty-four-hour convenience stores, or head home for a quick nap before the sun rises and their day jobs demand their attention. Beat-up Hondas and rusted-out Mitsubishis line the west side of Market Street, their owners either too brave or too poor for off-street parking. No one parks on the east side of the road tonight; posted signs threaten hefty fines for blocking the Wednesday morning street sweeper.

The night is clear and, if it weren't for the light pollution from a thousand streetlamps, Orion and Cassiopeia would twinkle through my Tiburon's moon roof. Tiburon means *shark* in Spanish, and the name fits. It never feels like I'm driving home from work each night but cutting my way through asphalt and sodium-vapor in a vast concrete ocean. Alice in Chains blares from the speakers and I feel like the predator after which my car is named.

The Tiburon growls as I downshift into the speed limit change, as if it's angry with me for slowing us down. We're halfway home, and Market Street is empty. Every traffic light is green, and the only other soul in sight is a dark figure a few blocks away, no doubt walking home from the bar. My foot taps with the music as the Tiburon and I make our way north.

The lone figure stops at the south corner of Market and MacArthur, and by now I can see it's a woman. She holds herself up against the streetlight and peers into the road at me and the Tiburon. She looks like she wants to cross against the light and is waiting to see if I'll stop and let her pass or speed through. My inclination is to speed through, but the light turns amber, so I hit the clutch, throw the transmission into neutral and stick my arm out the moon roof to wave her across. It's a simple gesture—direct—two flicks of the wrist toward the opposite corner.

I never learned the woman's name, but I like to think of her as Odessa. She reads my gesture and starts walking before my light is red. She has a hitch in her gait, as if one leg is shorter than the other, and each time she puts her weight on the short leg the rest of her body seems to twitch and shake in a kind of vertical seizure. Instead of crossing the street, however, Odessa lurches her way to my stopped car. Fear and paranoia aren't my thing, and only once have I consciously locked my car doors while driving. Before I realize what she's doing, Odessa opens the passenger door, slides into the leather bucket seat next to me and says, "Hey, Sugar, how ya doing tonight?"

". . . Fine . . . " I say, too shocked for much else.

The light turns green, but I don't move. Odessa smiles at me and drops a shaking hand onto my thigh. Her entire body twitches and jerks as if she's sitting on ten thousand volts and loving every minute of it. "You looking for some sugar, Sugar?"

For half a millisecond I'm flattered, as if she genuinely finds me attractive. For the other half I think I might accept her proposal (I am a man, after all), but reality sets in and my imagination takes over. If the open sores on her face and arms aren't a turn off, the kinds of sores I imagine I'll find elsewhere certainly are. I pull a fake smile and say, "Not tonight. But thanks anyway."

Odessa thrusts her jaw into a pout and turns toward the door. I think she's going to get out of the car, but she swipes a shaking hand under her nose and turns back to me. "Is you gay?"

I stifle a laugh. Maybe she truly believes the only reason a man would turn her down is because he's gay. I'm not above lying to spare someone's feelings . . . especially if it speeds up this entire series of events and gets me home to bed. I pull my mouth into the slant of unavoidable disappointment and shrug my shoulders. "Yeah," I say.

Odessa continues on as if I never spoke. "Ronnie stole all

my money, see," she says, picking at a scab on her arm. "I'm just trying to get some cigarettes, but the bastard at the Chevron won't sell me any. I was on my way to the 76 when you stopped."

I want to say, "I didn't stop for you," but instead I say, "Oh. Okay," and put the Tiburon in gear. The 76 Station was two blocks back the way I came, but if driving Odessa there would get her out of my car and me to bed, so be it.

I pull into the parking lot. A group of men huddle under the streetlight. They turn to look at us. "Here you go," I say.

Odessa opens the door and half climbs and half falls out. "Thanks," she says. "You're all right for a gay." Before she closes the door, however, she twitches and smiles and says, "You got any money?"

I sigh, reach into my pocket, and hand her a five dollar bill. "Here you go."

She grabs the bill. "Thanks again." She slams the door and walks. I glance back at the men huddled under the light. They're still staring at me. I drop my hand from the steering wheel, moving by inches—I don't want them to notice what I'm about to do. They're strangers to me, but I still seem to care what they think. I push down on the door lock and pray they don't hear it click.

As I pull away I whisper, "You are not a bigot," but from this day on I lock my doors each time I start the engine.

Poetry/Sonja Kosler

The Next Step Forward

Old is not a measure of time
but of quantity and distance.
How many burdens can one being carry
before youth erodes?
How many battles, banners, badges can one small person wear
before the heart wears and hardens?
How often can the road extend
before desire to reach the end explodes?
How far can the bigots, Babbitts, babblers detour the path
before it just plain disappears?
When does the next assault on the body become the last?
When is the next step forward the beginning of the past?
There comes a moment when the quantity and the distance
are become too great,
when the soul grows small and cold
and I am . . .
i am so very old.

Poetry/Deborah Rasmussen

Long Distance

Silence first. Then
the thread your voice has become
sews a seam between us.

> *It's Cathy.*
> *I'm calling to say goodbye.*

Never
have I held such words to my ear.

> *I expect to die soon.*
> *I'm ready.*

Someone, where you are,
holds the phone for you,
patiently dials numbers,
keeps your edges together
as you work the final stitches.

A moment hangs on the line
while I gather up my own edges,
bind them fast to yours.

> *I love you, Cathy.*

That's all.

After the call
I go to my closet,
find the shirt you embroidered
twenty-some years ago
and hold it.

Poetry/Susan Perala-Dewey

Honor Guard

Rest easy old turtle
Relax the body that has carried your shell across this land
Perhaps one hundred years

Already it has been one moon since I saw you on the
    roadside
Where hawkweed and daisy arch over your larger-than-life
    body
Seeking the full light of each long day

In your final moments, you flattened roadside grasses
Mowing your own cemetery toward the maple and poplar
    canopy
Near a stand of white pines, a short journey from the sandy
    riverbank

For more than a week you still looked strong enough to walk
    away
Now as raspberries ripen along with chokecherries and wild
    plums
Blueberry moon calls you home

All that's left is your sacred shell now graced by purple aster
As monarchs flutter above you in homage
Remembering your stories
Trails to peace between spirit worlds.

Fiction/James Robert Kane

Footprints on the Moon

She is happy, this little girl who dances uninhibitedly upon the footboard of my bed.

That much I know for sure. It is a pleasant change from the regular rabble gathering there. They all want something from me.

Not her. She chatters pleasantly, fresh from riding unicorns one night, leaving footprints on the moon the next. I look forward to her appearances, though I have no idea who she is or why she visits. I can't even describe her because she is more wisps of smoke than anything else, yet little girl nonetheless, because of her voice. She gives me no clues, makes no references to my life so that I might place her.

Yet I have this overpowering feeling that somehow she is part of me. Or me of her.

My wife knows none of this. She has slept soundly through each encounter, and right now I feel no need to tell her. I certainly won't tell my annoyingly clairvoyant daughter. She has been prescient about many things and steadfastly believes that I fathered a child in Vietnam. Exasperated protestations do not dissuade, so I will not add fuel by telling her about this ephemeral little girl.

I decide to ask my great uncle, the archivist of a family history that stretches from England to the first colonies and on to the Midwest, if our story might harbor mysterious progeny. None exist, he says, but in the recounting reveals a strange and relatively recent prohibition: no female born to the family shall be named Margaret.

I press. He takes off his glasses and wipes his eyes. He says that beginning with his grandmother, every daughter christened Margaret died within her first month, including his mother's sister. His own mother named her firstborn to honor that loss, and that baby perished as well. Then a cousin tragically tempted fate.

It makes me wonder if the little girl on my footboard is this oft-evicted soul. If so, she seems happy to be permanently relegated to the spiritual realm.

One night as she dances, I softly recite the name. Her aura turns slightly pink, as though she is blushing. She neither confirms nor denies as she abandons the dance to share secrets concerning fairy dust.

I continue to wonder who she is and occasionally dream that she is my spirit guide, come early to get acquainted. Perhaps she was my mother's, too.

It is a loving caress, this dream, its premise comforting. She knows the way home.

Poetry/Sawyer Johnson

For Guinevere

I see her in the
cheap Walmart sweaters of every
woman boarding the bus. She is in the
lining, stitched on the breast like a
patch of some kittens playing with yarn,
each of their whiskers a brown thread.
She is in these women's eyes, their sneakers, the
tired way their hair sits unbrushed around their shoulders.
My memories are greased by every curl.
I remember well the first time she ever
cut hers off. It had been long locks
fit for Queen Guinevere to pile atop her head before some
ball, to let Arthur undo in some
hushed hallway while guests
danced and clinked and laughed.
Before, it tumbled down her back
the way men tumbled off her like some big rock they
leapt from when they were young and didn't care.
Do they ever?
I see her in Guinevere's white marble
gravestone next to her husband's and in the harsh quiet of
how she will really be buried: alone.

Poetry/James Bettendorf

Onion Soup
—For Pat

Bent over a cutting board
an onion sharply diced
cotton apron faded
loosely tied, the bow
rests at the small
of her back

I announce my presence
        Your tears
are tears of gratitude, I said
for having so much to eat

        Rubbish
she whispered
tossed the chunks
into the pot
        we have no potatoes
no meat to thicken the broth

        But we have us
I said, ringing my arms
around her waist

        Rubbish
she said again
with a smile

Creative Nonfiction/Karen Kasland

The Last Visit

I wondered about bringing Molly to see him so often. I watched for signs she was reluctant, afraid or just sad. But she always skipped into the nursing home, taking the stairs to his room much too fast. She waited for me, scuffed sneakers bouncing impatiently on the edge of the landing.

Prancing to his chair and kissing his whiskered cheek, she startled him. He looked up at her, his great-granddaughter, with morning-glory blue eyes. Those eyes that could still twinkle—an honest-to-goodness twinkle—stood out in stark contrast to his altered, skeletal face, the skin stretched to a shine over protruding bones.

Most days I don't think he knew who we were, but he always seemed to know he *should* know us and was always pleased we were there.

The smell of him had changed and, nice as the place was, the odor of urine lingered. He railed against wearing pull-ups—"diapers" as he called them. At Christmas he had managed to sneak them into the collection bin for charity.

Food crumbs were rarely missing from his chin and clothes; his eyeglasses were usually broken; and one front tooth had been knocked out in a fall. None of that mattered to Molly.

While I settled in to talk with Grandpa, Molly dragged out the box of old toys brought from his house to this tiny apartment. She loved the rusty trucks, the plastic doll with ratty brown hair and green pajamas, and the blocks. They were the same wooden blocks her grandpa and her dad played with when they were her age.

"Have you heard from Patrick?" I asked.

"He got that job out in California," he said. "Rose is graduating from college. She's going to be a nurse."

These events happened over forty years earlier, but I enjoyed hearing about them and, on a good day, he enjoyed telling them.

On bad days, he seemed to know he couldn't remember his own life. He said little, and appeared angry and agitated. Watching Molly play eased his distress. Her almost constant singing also soothed him; his jaw relaxed and peace returned to his face.

He wagged his bony finger at her, made a mock-stern face and said, "Just what do you think you're doing?"

She looked sideways at him—her thoughtful look—laughed, and told him what she was building, and how the white plastic horse had to catch the green tractor with the man glued to its seat to warn him a storm was coming.

Our visits weren't long, but she gravitated to his chair often, to hold his hand or tell him something in a loud, slow, exaggerated way—a practice she learned to help him hear her. She didn't care one bit whether his responses made sense. Other times she simply stood beside him and stroked his arm with her plump, soft fingers. The contrast of her supple skin against his blotchy, blue-veined forearm was like a time-lapse photography trick.

Molly, named for his mother, noticed everything. On drives home she frequently paused, mid-song, to declare her observations that he looked skinnier, or his hands shook, or the skin under his eyes looked "more purpler." In her five-year-old wisdom, these were not things to fret about or fix. They were just the facts.

The last three days of Grandpa's life, he lay in a coma. Part of me wanted to bring her to him, so he could hear her voice. The other part, the part that prevailed, thought it might upset her too much. I wanted her to remember him as he was when she last saw him. When she kissed him goodbye that afternoon, he lifted his eyes from his worrying hands.

At the sight of her, he stopped mumbling, broke into a grin, waved, and said, "Bye-bye."

We cried a lot the day Grandpa died. We talked about missing him and loving him. We talked about his suffering being over. We thought about him being with Grandma and telling her all about the great-granddaughter she never met.

Later that evening, Molly went out on the back deck alone. It was already dark, and a clear night. When she came inside, I asked what she had been doing. She looked sideways at me—her thoughtful look—and said she sang a song for Great-Grandpa up in heaven, telling him goodnight. Then she skipped off to take her bath.

Poetry/Mary A. Conrad

Haiku

risking winds of love
the fledgling heart lifts, amazed
to discover wings

Poetry/*Honorable Mention*/Doris Lueth Stengel

Buried in the Past

My friend handed it to me
asked if I knew what it was—
this bruised piece of wood,
with a few flakes of white paint
hanging on, traces of red on the edge.

I trembled with memories.
She had placed in my hand
the knife holder from our kitchen.
She had laid my long-dead
mother in my palm.

When the old abandoned garage
near my childhood home was demolished,
my friend, who lived across the street
and played house with me
in the upper level of that garage,
found this artifact in the wreckage.

It had lost all scent of baking beans.
Carries no touch of soft bosom
as Mother daily braided my hair.
No quiet voice of gentleness.
Only this wood, past resurrection.

Dare I carry this soiled relic
to the cemetery, dig a small trench
near the gray granite stone,
place this long dead wood
near my mother's long dead hand.

Poetry/Arnie Johanson

Celebrating Our Anniversary, Without You

No balloons. No flowers. No music.
No waltz, no tango, no rock or roll.
Of course, there never was any of that
in previous years. We'd simply come here
to our favorite restaurant and share a meal,
you with shrimp and grits or crushed-almond
crusted trout, me trying to avoid the muddy glare
of my whole fish. I'd start with a martini
(you got to drive home) with salmon tartare,
sharing its companion sesame crisp
as we split a warm beet and spinach salad.

Tonight I'm having the trout, as is our daughter.
I devour the fish and see you sitting next to us
last fall, a wispy smile on your face made luminous
by the candle on the table reflecting off the white
kerchief over your radiation-balded head.
You knew it was your final restaurant meal
and were determined to wring the last bit
of enjoyment out of it.

I linger over my coffee, aware that the full dose
of caffeine will not sit well with the alcohol
and seafood, but I couldn't not have coffee
on our day. No second cup, however.
We step out into the cool March air.

Poetry/William Upjohn

Required Coursework

Shortly after Sam's death,
my widowed sister sits
at the dining room table
alone after dinner

doing her best to focus
on the task: to label
the limbic system's cerebral
structures for her class, *The Neuro-*

science of Emotions.
One of few courses not amended
in her cruel education
about abrupt life revision.

Fiction/Harlan Stoehr

Bus Tour To The Holy Land

At twenty-nine, Urho Katavouri stood five feet seven, weighed 157 pounds, had piercing blue eyes, thick dark hair like that of his male ancestors and, neatly dressed in khaki shirt and slacks and polished black shoes, operated Urho's Upholstery in Karstula, Minnesota.

Urho's Finnish grandparents emigrated to America in the late 1800s, homesteaded 160 acres near Karstula and raised seven children. Taivo, eldest son and Urho's father, inherited the farm, and there he and Lempi, his wife, raised three sons and two daughters.

Urho, youngest son, worked at various jobs around Karstula after high school until mustering courage to take the bus to Duluth, where he found work in an upholstery shop. Never comfortable in Duluth, always homesick, after four years he withdrew his savings, took a bus back to Karstula, bought a vacant blacksmith shop with a three-room apartment above, and converted it into an upholstery shop. He never married.

At 3:17 p.m. on a blustery Tuesday in November, while upholstering the rumble seat of a collector's 1931 Ford Model A Cabriolet in blue pinwale corduroy, Urho Katavouri felt the call to preach.

At 5:52 a.m. Wednesday, Urho Katavouri awoke from a dream of visiting The Holy Land.

At 10:23 a.m. Thursday, Toivo Makela, Karstula's butcher and pastor of its Apostolic Church, died of a heart attack.

At 9:30 a.m. Sunday, Urho Katavouri preached his first sermon.

As others of its kind, Urho's church was served not by an ordained seminary graduate, but by a layman who felt the call to preach and did so while continuing his vocation.

For many months, between his upholstery shop, part-time

job as substitute school bus driver, and preparing his Sunday service and sermon, Urho Katavouri's mind was fully occupied. Then, in various forms, usually after preaching on a New Testament text during the Lenten season, his Holy Land dream recurred. The more it returned, the more he yearned to make it real. Doing so would not be simple. For one thing, Urho feared the thought of flying. For another, the trip would be expensive. And money he saw little of.

Over the next three decades his congregation's membership varied from about thirty-seven to fifty-five, with half to two-thirds usually attending services. Through the years, as he baptized, married and buried his congregation, Sunday offerings were slim, the pastor's take minuscule. Though living frugally—his one extravagance an annual trip to the national church convention in Hancock, Michigan, over St John's Sunday weekend in June—Urho saved little toward a trip to The Holy Land.

Announcing his retirement on the thirty-fifth anniversary of preaching his first sermon, he confided in his congregation—thirty-nine attending that day—his long-held dream of the special trip and goal of accomplishing it in retirement. The congregation responded with a potluck dinner in his honor a week later, presenting him a purse of $473 to help achieve his dream. Given Urho's meager earnings and savings, travel prospects remained dim.

Then, while trolling the internet on Karstula Library's single patron-access computer, he found a site that quickened his pulse and stirred his imagination: Here was The Holy Land, re-created in Florida, near—of course—Orlando. He read in anticipation of its Dead Sea Qumran Caves, replicating those where Dead Sea Scrolls were discovered; the Wilderness Tabernacle; the Jesus boat replica of a boat dating to the time of Christ found in the Sea of Galilee; a complete model of Jerusalem in the year 66 AD, including the City Gate; the Calvary Garden tomb; and much, much more.

Here was the answer to prayer—opportunity to gain the

complete Holy Land experience without a pricey passport, the drudgery and dread of security lines, the tedious overnight overseas flight, the hassle of dealing with strange foreign currency, unfamiliar food, political unrest and concerns about drinking water. With a burst of inspiration not unlike his call to the ministry more than thirty-five years before, the retired Pastor Katavouri decided he would organize and lead a bus tour to The Holy Land.

His tour's first overnight stop would be Wartburg Seminary at Dubuque, Iowa, with its inspirational statue of Lutheranism Founder Martin Luther.

His second stop would be Golgotha Family Fun Park at Cave City, Kentucky, whose golf course's first nine holes are named for the first nine books of the Old Testament, and the eighteenth lies on a hill at the foot of a cross.

Third would be Dollywood at Pigeon Forge, Tennessee, because he considered Dolly Parton a good Christian woman, liked her music, and wished to see her habitat.

Next would be a day at Charleston, South Carolina, visiting historic churches. A day later his tour would reach The Holy Land. After two full days of exploring its wonders, the return to Minnesota would have but two overnights at motels.

Buoyed by his prospects and hoping to cover his own costs if enough prospects signed on, he printed a flyer announcing an informational meeting at his church and sent it to area churches of his kind. More than thirty came. Attendees showed interest, with three caveats: 1) that travel is in a real tour bus, not a school bus, 2) that the tour bypass Golgotha Family Fun Park and spend a second day at Dollywood, and 3) that the cost not be much more than the trips to Branson to which they were accustomed.

Undaunted, Urho detailed his route in a letter to each of three tour bus operators, requesting a price. Greatly dismayed by the quotes he received, all, he knew, far beyond the comfort zone of his prospects, he devised Plan B. Somewhere he would find a used tour bus to rent or buy and drive the tour himself.

His search began and ended at Karstula Library's computer, locating no bus for rent but, near Tioga, North Dakota, a used Farmers Union tour bus with 967,800 miles on its odometer for sale by its late owner's estate. A long-distance call yielded a heartening quote that he took to his bank, which agreed to finance half the cost of the bus.

Ten days later an acquaintance headed west on Highway 2 to visit Glacier National Park agreed to drop him at Tioga, where the estate administrator met him and drove him to the bus. Its paint was dim but tires sound, the diesel engine started quickly and, initial clatter subsided, ran smoothly. Upholstery was the downer, most of it shredded by rodents that had appropriated the bus for housing.

The administrator agreed to a sizable discount, noting in conversation that a reclusive goat rancher about thirty-five miles south of town had a quantity of tanned goatskin on his hands. Urho's upholstering instincts kicked in and, bus transaction signed and documents in hand, filled up with diesel at the Co-op and headed for the goat ranch.

In goat-keeper Karl Hofmeier, Urho Katavouri found a kindred spirit. At eighteen, Swiss-born Hofmeier inherited a substantial sum from an uncle, knew of North Dakota's vast space from reading of Theodore Roosevelt, and set out to see it for himself. Driving about, he found an isolated, woven-wire enclosed section and a half of land with a grove of trees, a well, small house, large barn, and good-sized machine shed for sale at an unbelievable price. He bought it, acquired male and female Toggenburg goats, popular in his native Switzerland, increased them, and lived happily alone with his goats for, now, forty years.

Goatskins Hofmeier had. Urho calculated his need and negotiated a price. They bundled the hides, warm from their storage spot beneath a hot steel roof, and loaded them into the bus's beneath-the-floor baggage compartment. Darkness approaching, Hofmeier invited Urho to stay for supper and the night. They visited companionably until past midnight.

After a breakfast of fried potatoes, goat sausage and eggs, Urho bade farewell to his new-found friend, started his bus, and drove away. Had he glanced back, he might have noted a sizable wet spot of ground where his bus had stood.

The early fall morning was unseasonably warm and still, prelude to an approaching storm, Urho thought, engrossed in driving and heedless to an increasingly heating bus floor. Rearview mirror now showing thick smoke rolling from beneath, he pulled his bus to the roadside, dismounted, and saw with dismay flames spreading rapidly beneath the bus toward its leaking fuel tank.

In minutes Urho was left with the clothes on his back, the bombed-out shell of a bus and hopelessly charred bundles of goatskins.

He set out on foot, five and a half sweaty hours later reaching a blacktop road.

Twenty minutes later a 1960s VW camper van, windows open, pulled up beside him. "Where you headed, friend?" its bearded, also '60s-vintage driver asked.

Urho's response was unequivocal: "Orlando, Florida, to The Holy Land."

Poetry/Janice Larson Braun

It's Time

The sun is pulling away from us.
No longer white hot,
His light is pale,
His caress tepid.
Like some indifferent lover
Who just a few months ago
Warmed our beds at night
And brought us ecstasy every morning,
He now is distant.

He sits at my table,
Picking at his salad—
Fingers restless
Thoughts elsewhere.
He thinks about the hills of New Zealand,
The beaches of South Africa,
And something new and exotic
On the streets of Rio.

Finally, I fold my napkin carefully
On the table,
Look him directly in the eye
And ask,
"How long will you be gone?"

Poetry/Chet Corey

First Morning

How she'd place her hand—
fingers webbed out wide
as if in blessing over the crown
(that soft spot of a newborn)
without touching its thinnest hair,
the head's moist heat rising up
toward her opening palm—
and feel along her nightstand,
dresser top or bathroom vanity
where her dentures (She'd say,
My teeth) soaked overnight
in a half-full glass of Efferdent.
And then feel along end tables,
kitchen table, or the dresser top
until she'd found her glasses.
That was how she webbed out her
fingers across clean bed linen—
in that way I'd seen, seated beside
her on the piano bench, those
fingers flare from middle C to C—
she half-awake that morning,
our father from her world gone.

Poetry/Arnie Johanson

Pieces

I picked up the pieces of the blue ceramic bird
that crashed to the floor when lightly brushed
by a slightly tipsy dinner guest whose apologies
were much too repetitious, much too gushy to be real.

The bird was one of three I'd purchased
as a child, a present for my mother
paid for with my first ten dollars ever earned.
I got them back when Mother died.

I don't know what my mom would think of me
today, at seventy-five a chronic wine consumer
who never reads his Bible, never prays (well, nothing
she would recognize as prayer), and writes

and writes poems that she would surely find
had far too many awful words, providing
far too little Christian inspiration, although
she'd only say they are far too deep for her.

The bird was broken into two, her tail
separated from the rest of her. An easy fix.
A drop or two of super glue, she'd be intact
again and nobody would ever know.

Two decades have passed. The pieces remain,
buried in some box or dresser drawer. The other
birds lie with her, waiting for me to find the nerve
to glue things back together.

Fiction/*Honorable Mention*/Edis Flowerday

The Great Minnesota Get-Together

James had gone to the State Fair every year since he was a boy, and he loved the ritual of it, the way it marked the end of summer and the start of an energizing autumn. Emma, his wife, felt differently. "It never changes," she'd say. "And, when we go, we do the same things in the same order year after year after year." That Saturday morning as they rode the express bus to the fairgrounds, she went further. "The sheep and the pigs and the cows and all those lop-eared bunnies. What a yawn! Then there's the state's biggest boar, stretched out in his pen sound asleep. Double yawn!" She sat quietly for a few minutes before going on in a milder tone. "I *am* fascinated by those crazy chickens though, the ones with feathers sticking straight up on their heads, like something out of Dr. Seuss. And I *will* give you the horses. Beautiful animals and so strong. But that Miracle of Birth thing? Gives me the creeps!"

James could agree with that last observation. Once they'd gone in and spent over two hours waiting in vain while a cow in labor roamed the enclosure, casually munching the feed that was strewn about. A couple of young men armed with cameras sat on wooden stools, waiting to record the action, and it looked like they'd be there for a long, long time. "This is disgusting," James said. "Even a cow needs a little privacy." And so they left. Farm animals popping out one baby after another only reminded him that he and Emma had failed to reproduce. He was sure it wasn't his fault; so sure, in fact, that he refused to get it checked out.

As their bus neared the fairgrounds, Emma proposed a plan. "Let's do things differently this year. You go to the Art Building on your own, and I'll check out Creative Activities. We can spend as much time as we like. And then at noon we'll meet for lunch at the Food Building. After that we can roam around together."

Well, why not? Emma never got into the art that much, and he couldn't see the point of all that patchwork and weaving and home-canned fruit. It was a good idea. So he went to the art display and was enjoying it at a leisurely pace. That is, until he got to the photograph of the man and the woman tooling along on a motorcycle. The man drove, staring straight ahead, looking bored, as if he'd rather be home in front of the TV with a beer, watching the baseball game and falling asleep when the innings got slow. His mustache was in serious need of grooming, as was his long, low ponytail. On his forearm, he sported a tattoo of an American flag. He was what James would call a smug, self-satisfied man.

The woman, however, looked poised and cultured, an entirely different type. She wasn't hanging on to the guy the way a woman usually did on a motorcycle, her arms circling his waist, her face nuzzling the back of his neck. She rested her hands on her thighs and sat up straight. Her blond hair was in a bun with a few stray wisps blowing across her face, partially obscuring it. It was a look of casual disarray, like the one Emma tried to achieve every morning before heading off to work at the downtown library. The woman's head was turned only slightly toward the camera, while she gazed off into space with just the hint of a smile, a little like Emma's smile when she did Tai Chi. And then James leaned in for a closer look. The woman wasn't just *like* Emma. She *was* Emma! Emma on a motorcycle with a tattooed guy! James turned to the couple standing next to him. "That's my wife!" he blurted out. They smiled nervously and moved off.

And now Emma was on her own for a couple of hours at the State Fair. The Great Minnesota Get-Together. That's how they advertised it. And she had maneuvered being alone in the Creative Activities Building. Did she expect this motorcycle guy to ooze out from behind one of the hand-quilted coverlets and lead her off to the Midway where he'd win a giant Teddy bear in proof of his masculine prowess? Or maybe they'd meet at the Giant Slide and go down sitting on the same gunny sack, her tush firmly planted between his widespread legs, his arms locked around her while she threw back her head and shrieked like a girl. Despite her limited interest in the animal barns, they might go there where things got basic and suggestive and odorous. If Emma suddenly turned up pregnant after all James's loving but ineffectual efforts, he'd have to kill this guy. Then he'd be in jail for the rest of his life. James checked the title of the photograph. "Alone Together." Clever. Was there a sequel? "Together Alone."

James rushed to the Creative Activities Building and began a frantic search. The place was a labyrinth, displaying, among other things, hand-tailored clothing, caps and mittens knit from homespun goat hair, and chairs and tables cobbled together in basement workshops during long winter evenings. There were dead ends everywhere. It was claustrophobic. At one point he stumbled into a gaggle of teenaged girls gawking at strapless gowns designed with a sock monkey motif. Sock monkey heads dotted hemlines and defined waists. Sock monkey heads even formed bra cups. "This is just so cool," one girl said. "Wouldn't you love something like that for prom?" James gave her a horrified look and raced off. The girls all laughed.

Once outside, he dialed Emma on his cell phone, but she wasn't picking up. Well, of course not. She had other things on her mind. He headed to the Midway where he ran smack into the big noise of grinding engines and the shrieks of people being whipped around on the rides. Pausing briefly, he glanced to his right in time to see a little boy throw up a shocking pink liquid while his mother said, "Well, *that* was a waste of four dollars." James's head began to throb; and, when the boy blew upchuck out of his nostrils, James bent over and lost what was left of his breakfast

He recovered slightly and tried to calm himself. *She likes horses*, he thought. *I'll check the Hippodrome.* But he couldn't get in. Teams of Clydesdales were inside pulling their painted wagons around, and he needed a ticket. After wandering aimlessly, he came to the Horticulture Building. Emma loved flowers, especially dahlias. Maybe she was in there looking for a new variety. Or maybe she was checking out the Crop Art. That always struck her as funny and satirical. But James could not find her. Dejected, he gave up and went to wait in front of the Food Building, where he flopped down on a bench.

When Emma found him, she took one look, and asked,

"Are you having one of your migraines? Are you seeing double?"

"Maybe." He put a hand over one eye and then over the other. "Yep, definitely seeing double. There's two of you."

"Stay here," she said. "Maybe you're just hungry. I'll get us a couple of those wild rice burgers."

"See if they have any roasted turkey legs. I feel like walking around gnawing on something substantial, tearing the flesh off the bone."

Emma came back with two burgers and two iced teas. She kept a close eye on James while he ate. When he finished, he stood and said, "There's something I want you to see over in Fine Arts."

"Okay," she said. "I'm game. I'll say one thing for Fine Arts. They've got a decent Ladies Room over in one corner. And there's never much of a line."

When he had her in front of the photograph, she squealed. "Oh, I meant to tell you that'd be here! Audrey took it last June." Audrey was their neighbor. "The guy's connected to her daughter somehow. He was driving his Harley coast-to-coast and stopped here on the way. I got a ride to the corner and back. What a kick! The interesting thing is that Audrey almost never takes pictures. Leaves that to the hubby. She couldn't believe it when this shot got into the fair. Costco did the blowup."

"Let's go home," James said.

"Really? But I haven't seen a single politician yet. Haven't had a chance to shake hands. You know, press the flesh. And I'd like some dessert. You know how I feel about deep-fried ice cream. It's like Baked Alaska on a stick."

The mere thought of it made James feel queasy again. "Spare me the details," he said. And he headed for the door.

Poetry/Ryan M. Neely

A Prose Author's Misunderstanding of Poetry

Poets
Read lines
With syrup voices
No matter the subject
Be it flowers or rape

Dramatic pauses
In lieu
Of proper punctuation
Are meant
To add gravitas
To otherwise
Lifeless words

When I
Listen to poets
I insert
Tension and drama
By imagining
William Shatner
Reading their lines

If I
Listen close
I half expect
To hear
"My God
Spock
What do we do?"

Poetry/Georgia A. Greeley

My Last Night Out

She stormed past me out the door,
not pausing to be paid.
I barely snagged her arm in passing.
She looked behind me into the house
and her words flamed like wildfire:
"Amy was bobbing for apples in the toilet
I barely got her cleaned
and found Paddy
had overturned every potted plant in the house;
I was cleaning up that mess
when I heard repeated *thunks*
coming from the kitchen;
Jimmer had found a butcher knife—
he was standing on the table chopping up
an unopened loaf of bread.
I screamed. Sat them all on the couch
and told them not to move until bedtime."
She yanked her arm out of my grip
and stared me down.
"Three children under five," she yelled.
"What were you thinking?
I'm never going to get married!"

She almost ran down the sidewalk.
I watched her disappear in the summer dusk,
fairly certain I'd lost my only babysitter.

Poetry/Sandra Melchisedech Burwell

Now I'll Cut the Grass

She pushed in the choke,
Put the gearshift into high,
Held the safety bar.
Pulled the cord.

It stuck,
It clicked,
Then nothing.

She let go of everything.
Reset it all and started over.
Stick,
Click;
Then nothing.

Check the gas.
Straighten the wheels.
Make sure it's on level ground.
Pull the cord again.
Stick, click, then nothing.

Three strikes and you're out
Time for a nap.

Her life was like a lawn mower that wouldn't start
Full of the ability to do great things,
Except at the time of delivery.

Poetry/Pagyn Alexander

First Kiss

My first kiss happened
on a kindergarten playground
three months after my fifth birthday.

I can't recall his name,
but remember instead dark eyes,
tiny corkscrew curls, and caramel skin,
the soapy scent of my new best friend
in her frilly dress,

and how we linked arms when we ran
grabbing him from behind
spinning him around
almost falling down
as we planted
sloppy kisses on his cheeks.

We twirled away, laughing
like those grown-up girls
we'd seen on the big screen.

Breathless, we leaned
our backs against a tree
not saying a word,
sucking on candy cigarettes
until the school bell rang.

Freshman Initiation
Thanksgiving, 2015

The first indication of significant change was son-in-law Steve's off-hand comment to the assembled family after he checked the electric heaters in the bunkhouse.

"You boys better move your beer farther from the bunkhouse door. You're going to pee on it when you get up in the night," he said.

My sweet grand boys . . . no matter their broad shoulders and deep voices . . . my sweet grand boys brought beer? I had filled the garage refrigerator with Gatorade and bottled root beer—their favorite drinks. And I was anxious to hear about the two college boys' first semester at the University.

"You boys brought your own beer?" An auntie laughed.

"Ya, we did," they said with bravado. "Busch Lite 'cause that's all college kids can afford."

Lord, put your arm around my shoulder and your hand over my mouth.

My little boys had apparently observed and fully understood the family obligations. The Phillips kids always arrive with coolers of food and meat and drink. Our daughters compete for refrigerator space, texting each other on the way to the lake—*We are turning off the highway onto the lake road. I am going to get the refrigerator first.*

This is the Hallmark card family that gathers at Camp *Ohana* (family) on the lake. This is the *ohana*—three daughters, their husbands, seven grandkids—I've written about for years. You know them from my stories about our gifts of time and talent. Instead of Christmas gifts, everyone performed. The girls danced one year, wrote and produced a play another. The boys wore cowboy hats and sang Toby Keith's "I Want to Talk About Me." In the first years, they were all taking piano lessons and plunked away on a keyboard. Later, they performed horn duets with their mothers at the keyboard.

You read about our Christmas in Disneyland—seven grandkids, thirty pieces of luggage, the granddaughter who spent Christmas Eve in her room sobbing because she didn't believe Santa would find her in California.

I've shared photos and stories about our winter campfires on the pond—hot dogs and s'mores, ice skating and playing hockey. You know these kids from our annual pig roast, and from the luau they hosted on our fiftieth wedding anniversary. The precious little boys wore lei and grass skirts and danced the hula with their female cousins.

These boys have always been pantry thieves. For years they grabbed handfuls of cookies from the pantry cookie jar and sneaked back to the television in the loft where food was not permitted. They also filled their pockets with peanut M&M's from Papa's stash in the pantry refrigerator. He refilled the supply regularly, and we all smiled with amusement at their naiveté.

This Thanksgiving a grandson was observed, and not with parental amusement, slinking out of the pantry on the way to the loft with a bottle of Papa's Pale Ale in each pocket.

"Idiots," twenty-year-old granddaughter Sarah remarked. "Freshmen boys are idiots."

Some erosion of our traditions had taken place over the years. One Christmas the grandkids—boys and girls—said NO to the gift of time and talent. They were done performing. One summer the grand boys said NO to the 4th of July lake parade. They were not wearing stupid costumes and carrying flags on a pontoon. We left them at the dock. They waited until we had cruised down the lake, then they got in the fishing boat and weaved in and out of the parade shooting at us and other parade boats with water guns.

There was another indication of grandkids changing from innocent children and obedient teenagers to rebels. After they left on the 4th of July weekend, I decided to give the bunkhouse a good cleaning. I dragged my 1957 graduation-gift Samsonite from under the bunk bed. When I opened it, instead of hats and old prom gowns for dress-up play, I found rockets and firecrackers.

In spite of their relentless gang-type nagging all weekend, their parents had firmly banned fireworks. We would attend the city fireworks display as we had for years. Better. Safer. Less expensive. The grandkids gave in. We went to the city fireworks. But later that weekend they were permitted to make their first excursion into town by themselves. There they pooled their resources, bought fireworks, and stashed them under the bed in the bunkhouse. Their plan was to light up the winter holidays.

A pile of campfire ashes is all that's left of the Thanksgiving holiday now. I did hear about the first semester in college around that campfire—somewhat swaggering information about girls and great parties, little enthusiasm for their classes despite my hungering questions about academics.

"Semester tests coming up?" I asked.

"There's this free day," one of them said. "I think finals are right after that."

Lord . . . your hand on my mouth.

Neither college boy had a final exam scheduled in Freshman Composition. "That course is a stupid waste of time anyway," they said. I was appalled. In the good old days, we made Freshman Comp a rigorous course. And in more recent days, my grand boys would not have expressed a negative thought of that sort to the Grammar Police.

Oh yes, in addition to the two gallons of milk and all that root beer left over in the refrigerator, I found a half bottle of Fireball in the freezer.

Poetry/Georgia A. Greeley

The Substitute

She walked in as if lost,
turned to check the door number,
turned back to us, and looked more lost
35 children + 1 teacher = 36

Every time she turned her back
to write on the blackboard,
35 desks and chairs crept quietly
towards the front of the room.
35 chairs + 35 desks = 70

When she had 7 long division problems
carefully chalked out,
and turned to ask for volunteers,
she was surrounded—unable to move.
I had never seen a teacher cry before.

The principal yelled and lectured
and stared each student down,
as we replaced every desk and chair just so.
35 children -1 teacher = principal
(the principal being a negative number).

Even at age twelve (7 + 5),
I knew I didn't ever want to teach seventh grade.

Poetry/Susan Coultrap-McQuin

Boys on Bikes

Circling again and again,
one tall, another squat
draped across handlebars
as they chatter and laugh.

Chasing, racing, circling
to fill the last day of summer,
to feast on free air
before the first day of school.

Their voices reach me
each time before they do,
circling the neighborhood
to savor summer's end.

Again and again they return
like summer birds,
circling our feeder
before their long flight south.

Poetry/Doris Lueth Stengel

Cooking up a Career

My college education interrupted
by romance and Happy-Ever-After dreams,
turned into fourteen years
of peeling and chopping classes,
slicing and dicing credits,
blending together an English degree.

The teaching career boiled
down to part-time subbing
by arrival of three children
looking for Mom and cookies
as they popped in the door
after school and play.

The poetry-writing fervor
bubbling in a kettle
pushed to a back burner,
stirred occasionally,
simmered to a rich broth
flavored by hugs and cookie crumbs
and endless revisions.

Not quite the flavor I planned,
but a satisfying soup after all.

Poetry/René Bartlett Montgomery

The Forecast

Winter returned overnight.
I find myself in hostile snow,
no plow in sight
wondering how
to set this right.

It's just a spring snow—
enough injustice to damage
delicate petals
but not the roots
we created together.

Just a spring snow—
angry words carried
on Alberta clippers
blowing judgment without justice
icy flakes in my face.

This frigid blanket
swathing the space between us
blows hard to justify its own existence
but we both know it won't last long—
no accumulation in the forecast.

But today
my heart is buried
and the icy thaw
fizzling in guilt and sprinting judgments
seeks justification in the cold.

Poetry/Kathryn Medellin

Autumn Morning

I feel the coolness
as I stroll
past morning glories
blossoms tightly closed
in their night's sleep.
Rising sun sends rays
across the sky
painting the edges
of wispy clouds
yellow and orange.
The lane
framed with
autumn flowers,
golden rod
plumes held high
on hairy stems,
purple asters
nod in a passing breeze,

red and white clover
spray sweet scents
across the meadow
filled with dew,
brown grass spikes
stand tall
above yellow foxtail.
A gold finch calls
Per-chik-o-ree
Per-chik-o-ree.
On my return
morning glories
have awakened
trumpeting
the morning.

Poetry/Shirley Ensrud

Ancestry

I close my nineteenth century novel—
Europeans in steerage struggling to survive
bad water, rats, rotten food and contempt—
to stay alive to arrive in America.

Eighty-year-old photo of myself
in the eighth year of my existence—
sitting on a velvet stool as an Aunt
clicked the lens—smiles at me.

Beside me, my ten-year-old spouse,
innocent as I, catches my eye
as he did, in person, twelve years later.
Wedding pictures of our parents flank us.

This gallery graces my office in our
Independent Senior Living apartment.
I reflect on my parents' large family,
nurtured during the depression,

his family surviving the unpredictability
of his father's heart and early death.
As newlyweds we worked hard,
raised three daughters.

With more love than finances, we existed
in this Utopia through World Wars, good times
and bad. Lived well enough, saved for retirement,
enjoyed trips to Britain, Hawaii, Europe,

now enjoy our four-score years thanks
to ancestors who often endured ocean voyages
of bad water, rats, rotten food and contempt
to plant their seeds and opportunities for us.

Poetry/Rosemary Vaughn

The Milkman Cometh

The milkman comes at dawn each winter's day.
He calls to horses plodding through the snow.
They stop and nod their heads and gently neigh,
While steam through harnessed frosty noses blows.
The milkman jumps down from the wagon door
Onto the path that leads to snowy steps.
Three "dead soldiers" await there as before—
To swing and clank from Johnny's old biceps.
Now Christmas Eve when Johnny comes at dawn,
Another "soldier" waits for Johnny's hand,
A full one, bronze with fire and ribbon on.
One "dead soldier" later, his favored brand,
The horses nod their heads and turn to go,
To take him safely homeward through the snow.

Creative Nonfiction/Joni L. Danzl

Air Mattresses

Heck, it's so hot we've decided to have a drink on the patio. Screwdrivers made with tangerine juice. Sun is getting much hotter. Our RV trailer is air conditioned and we've closed the blinds to keep out the sun. But who wants to sit inside? We sit inside all week at work. So we lounge outside in our lawn chairs, sipping our drinks, a Kenny Burrell CD playing. Nothing but trees and the lake below us. Plenty of ice in these luscious drinks. Let's go down and see if it's time for floating.

We saunter down the shady trail and scuff along the beach. The water is calm and no clouds in sight. Not many people around. "Yep, let's run up and grab our air mattresses." We find them stacked behind the trailer, last year's leaves stuck to them, muddy water in the cup holders. "But they're not bad! They need a little more air though, John," I say. He fires up the electric air pump.

I race to my closet and put on my trailer swimsuit. Kenny Burrell is still strumming. I'm a bit tipsy. I want to get down there before clouds come rolling in. But there's so much to do and space is limited. Lighting is poor. I find the cups that fit the cup holders. I dig out ice, vodka, tangerine juice, hat, sunglasses, towels, phones, keys. With a countertop the size of a cribbage board, it isn't easy. Our ninety-pound dog Russell is underfoot. I slather on sunscreen as mosquitoes gather on my back. The air conditioning rattles at top speed. It'll keep Russell cool while we're in the water. Finally I spring out of the trailer and hang my AT THE BEACH sign on the door. Lock up. Run down lugging my stuff, my air mattress dangling on my back.

There's John already on his air mattress lapping up the sun! I clamber onto my mattress and paddle out. The water is soft and barely cool. Wild roses bloom in shade along the shore. Their fruity scent muddles with the fragrance of tangerine and sunscreen. There's a poufy breeze and the current rocks us a

little. Two loons—regulars in our bay—skim the water, simply
playing. They're not even feeding, just lolling. It seems they do
that when it's hot. John is lolling too, carried on a slight current,
as though he were one of those sleek and silky loons.

Poetry/Mike Gainor

Fisher

Words are wily
Twist under your finger
Unhooked worms

Poetry
Is casting a net into the darkness
Into the dark darkness

And when
And if
That net twitches

We are not cowards
     not cowards

To fear
What we'll drag out

Poetry/Sandra Sidman Larson

What a Hike has to Teach Us

The talk of the river
runs beside us

as we meander toward
the lake, its misty vapors

stretching into early morning air,
the Sawtooth Mountains,

a backdrop to what comes into view.
We climb through its foothills,

through salmon-skinned birches
through yellow-flamed aspens

the woods rising
higher and higher in front of us

until the mountain ridges
appear, and we are struck

with silence as the forest
below us flares up in full view.

For once we are not rushing
past the red-veined leaves

that spread their colors around us.
For once we are not pressing on.

For once we absorb the moment of
all that spills out into this morning.

For once what is here
is enough.

Poetry/Joni Norby

Fishing for Sunnies

The fish flops and fights.
It's not Elizabeth Bishop's
Tremendous Fish—it's a Sunny.
A Pumpkinseed with her
bright orange spot on full display.
She weighs no more than
a pound, yet a wild tussle
ensues. Florescent scales
of olive-green to brown
to bright orange and blue
reflect the noonday sun.
Spiky fins and slippery
scales make her hard to grasp
as she wiggles to be free of me,
to jump back into the
water, to earn a do-over.
I carefully remove the hook,
grimy earth worm gone,
as her dead eye stares,
mouth in a frown.
She took the bait so easily,
hardly a minute gone
before my bobber bobbed.
With one tug she was hooked,
then pulled
from the depths of
Lake Pomme de Terre.
I keep my gaze on this Sunny,
one of Rilke's once-and-no-mores;
as I plop her in my net, I tell her
let go, we all must, and
I bait my line again.

Creative Nonfiction/Rosemary Vaughn

My Son, My College Roommate

It was a dark, cold November night on the northern plains as I drove the ninety miles to my home. My husband wasn't expecting me, so I called him on my antiquated flip phone. When he picked up, I blurted out, "I'm running out of cell battery, so I can't talk. I'm on my way home. Our son kicked me out of the apartment." I hung up.

As I drove along, snow drifting across the highway obscuring the yellow lines, I reflected on what had transpired over the last few days. The events tickled my funny bone, making me chuckle.

That fall, our son had returned to his home state to attend Medical School. I was already on campus, working on my doctorate and teaching classes, quite possibly part of the reason he escaped to an out-of-state school to attain his undergraduate degree and a little independence. I had told him upon his return that I would pay his living expenses if I could stay a couple of nights a week and on the weekends when his father and I were in town for the college hockey games. He readily agreed, and we became "college" roommates.

A colleague and I frequented the coffee house on campus, a popular spot for faculty and students alike. As it happened, my son was attracted to an undergraduate student who worked there. He suggested I put in a good word for him next time I ordered my Almond Roca Mocha. This proposal sounded a little too much like high school. A few days later, however, I found myself at the coffee shop counter and, against my better judgment, I casually mentioned to the familiar barista in the presence of said dream girl that I had a son on campus and he was available.

I thought he'd be pleased with my efforts on his behalf. Unfortunately, a few days earlier, unknown to me, he had already asked her out. Now he was mortified and chastised me for making it sound like I was trying to sell him off to the highest bidder. As a result, I was temporarily banned from the coffee shop.

That scenario precipitated the events of this dark and stormy night. I wasn't usually in town on a Thursday evening, but my husband was coming the next day for the Friday night hockey game, so it made more sense for me to stay than to turn around and come back the next day. I spent the early evening doing some Christmas shopping. Arriving back at the apartment, I was looking forward to my "jammies" and an evening of Hallmark Christmas movies on TV.

Balancing my shopping bags, I unlocked the door and had barely entered when a voice from the bathroom, yelled, "Mum!" followed by my son charging out of the bathroom, his wet hair indicating he'd just had a shower. He urged, "You have to get out of here!"

Stunned, I stared at him, my shoulders drooping from the weight of my parcels and the vision of my relaxing evening dissipating. The first date with "coffee girl" had been successful, so that evening they were going to a movie. My son reasoned that, since she had invited him in after their first date, he should reciprocate and, therefore, I shouldn't be there.

We had already had a few discussions about how awkward it was to show guests around the apartment when the tour revealed my frilly bedroom and the floral blue and pink rocker in the living room. Assuming he was afraid female friends would think he had a female live-in, I helpfully suggested he just tell them they were his mother's things. He looked at me incredulously. "Seriously? That helps a lot." Hmmm. A twenty-three-year-old young man living with his mother. Okay. I got it. Even his male friends might raise a few eyebrows at that one.

I caved, but where was I to go? Tired as I was, it seemed logical to just pack my overnight bag and go home. My son carried my bag to the car saying, "Thanks, Mum, for understanding."

I looked him straight in the eye and announced, "You owe

me—big time."

So, these were the circumstances bringing me to a late night drive on a desolate highway with drifting snow. Thinking my husband must be worried sick about my driving so late and wondering what could have happened, I was shocked to drive up to a house all in darkness. Even Tom Bodett, the spokesman for Motel 6, would leave the light on for you.

As I walked down the hallway to our bedroom, I could hear a low rumbling. He was already asleep. My amusing anecdote would have to wait until morning. My husband had always said he left the worrying to me because I did such a good job of it.

The bathroom light was on when I awoke the next day. My husband was shaving in preparation for work. Realizing I was awake, he poked his foam-frosted face around the door jam and demanded, "What the hell happened last night? Do I need to go over there and throw the kid and all his stuff out into the street? " Guess he was a little bit worried.

Chuckling, I related the events to him. He saw the humor in it, too, and joined in my amusement. I had learned many years ago that how I presented our kids' behavior and misadventures to their father affected his response to them. As the sweatshirt imprint states, "If Mama ain't happy, ain't nobody happy!" So this mama always tried to keep her cool and sense of humor when acting as the bridge between father and child.

My husband and I returned to the campus that evening, and the three of us enjoyed the hockey game. My son's little romance fizzled shortly after that, and I was allowed back in the campus coffee shop.

Poetry/Jennifer Hernandez

Twenty-five Below

with wind chill. Frostbite
can occur in fifteen minutes
to skin exposed.

You're in Minnesota now.
Dress warm.
Take care.

School canceled
due to dangerously
cold temps.

Back home in Ghana
did you cancel classes
for excessive heat?

Relentless sun beating
down. School uniform
stifling. Globules of sweat.

I don't know why
they called off school.
It isn't so cold, she says

in her mellifluous
voice with a disdainful
shake of black braids.

The rest of us bundled like marshmallows,
still complaining, sharp scrape of icy air
raking our cheekbones.

Poetry/Yvonne Pearson

Graduation Open House

The lace of lilacs tumbles
from the crystal vase.
Every spring
since I have lived
in my own house
I bring this fleeting bounty
to my bedroom.
The flower of brides.

This year I bring
the entire tree inside,
fill my house with
lavender lilacs
purple lilacs
lilac scent
cascading from piano, table, glass, and tile
more fragile than lilies
more fleeting than roses.
The flower of babies
and old women.
I fill my house today
with riotous beauty,
lilac bursting open the season.

It's the day we celebrate her leave-taking.
We lay out strawberries, cream cheese, watermelon, wine.
We lay out stories, paintings, and old photos:
one of my belly swelling welcome

> > >

under cotton flowers, me still sole owner of the girl;
one of her tulip head cradled in her father's palm;
one of our girl feeding her baby brother;
our girl naked under walnut tree. Slowly the scenes change.
She preens for the first dancing party,
hugs friends, climbs the Grand Canyon,
builds habitat houses;
she's wrapped in lavender chiffon and white prom roses.

We lay out toffee cookies and tea ring,
we lay out brownies and welcome
to a hundred people who cannot help us
as we lay out our swelling godspeed hearts
and I bring lilacs to her bedside table,
a first bouquet for her,
the fragrance filling the room
she prepares to leave.

Poetry/Sharon Chmielarz

End of Winter Crabapples

Suddenly magic in the crabapple tree's blueprint of sticks—
twenty-one robins, five waxwings and a pine finch

helicopter in, marauders in a rite of late
winter siege, a feasting called *staying alive.*

Bawdy and lusty and hungry and horny
probably, they barge into the tree's wattled rooms,

plucking and nipping, beaking and nudging,
warming their bellies by nibbling dark flesh

as if the tree were an old madam's whorehouse.
I counted them more than once, in all,

twenty-seven birds, full of banter. The tree
did not let them leave as famished virgins.

Poetry/Margaret M. Marty

Ode to Weeds

Brown-eyed Susans
sway in the breeze
on their tall stems
in roadside ditches.

Purple, blue, white gentian
signal the end of summer,
grace the perimeter
of yards and fields.

Not to be outdone,
rich goldenrod
seems to grow denser
year by year.

I took a long way home,
drove slowly along
the country roads,
drinking in the beauty—

some might call them weeds.

Poetry/Kit Rohrbach

Nightshade

I
Dawn is unknown to me.
When I rise,
the sun is long risen.
There are no pale pinks,
light blues, soft yellows
in my box of crayons.
Those were melted down
for candles
years ago.

II
I found them like that:
one crow feather fallen
chatoyant by moonlight;
a single purple nightshade
not planned or planted.
One dark vine
forced up through asphalt
in an alley,
one black quill
shed by chance
to slant against it.

III
Broken glass glitters
where the bricks
of the back of the bar
meet the blacktop
of the parking lot,
brown, green,
shining clear and sharp
smelling of old piss
and stale beer.
There is no story to it,
no drama, no poetry
of love and loss.
Just a toss
toward the dumpster,
a toss and a miss.
That is sad enough.

Poetry/Nicole Borg

Stealing the Dream

The girl runs across the mall parking lot,
black hair streaming, pumping arms clutching
Hollister Tees, two hundred dollar jeans,
Coach bag. Behind her the big man
his starched uniform, tinny badge,
sweating brown face. He has stopped shouting.

Across the parking lot stage,
lungs on fire, legs threatening to cramp,
she eyes the cottonwoods beyond the service road.
She worries the fabric of a T-shirt
like beads on a rosary.
Mary, mother full of grace,
Mami will kill me if I get caught.
Vamonos idiota. Corre. Corre.

She sprints past cars stopped in the road,
audience of mothers and towheaded kids
pointing—windows down, sunlight in.
They make no offer; back to their
regularly scheduled lives.
She runs, helps herself.

The mall cop huffs, but doesn't close the gap.
Stop running, Hija. You can't outrun
this sort of thing. Minimum wage jobs
and broken promises. After school
and nobody home.
He knows,
whether he catches her or not
he loses.
Whether she gets away or not
she loses.

Creative Nonfiction/Sharon Harris

Electronic Entertainment

I was at my kitchen desk the other day, paying bills. I was amazed at how much I was paying for communication, convenience, and electronic entertainment. I did some quick calculations. I was paying over one third of my paycheck on this stuff!

I paid a regular phone bill for the house phone, a long distance phone bill, a cell phone bill, and, lo and behold, a bill for the second phone line for the Internet. Then I also had a satellite dish bill. These bills were mainly for ease of communication, some of it disguised as entertainment.

Wasn't this rather extravagant?

You know, it wasn't all that many years ago that people had to walk or take a horse and buggy just to go talk to someone.

I know we've come a long way since the Pony Express days, but we have gone a bit overboard. We don't want to wait a few weeks to send a check and an order form in the mail and wait for an item to come back to us in the mail. Oh, no. That's not good enough. That's not fast enough. We have to phone in the order, use a credit card (going deeper into debt, by the way), and then pay for Express Mail, just so we can get the item a few days earlier. Well, we've gotten along without this particular item for quite some time. What are a few extra days? But no, we have to save time. Or, we phone in the order and have it charged right out of our checking account, giving out our bank account number and routing number. Or, we go out on the Internet and order it there, again giving out our credit card numbers or bank account numbers, sending them out into the void, just trusting on dumb luck that someone won't grab them and use them.

I remember watching Star Trek years ago. They had a talking computer that everyone thought would never happen. Well, they are not even unusual now.

Most of our life is spent on the telephone. The other employees at work don't recognize me without a phone growing out of my ear.

And again, in a work setting, the mail is not fast enough. We have to fax or scan documents to get information there even quicker. What did we ever do without email? And just what are we doing with all this time we are saving?

All these things at work are now infiltrating my personal life. Now I have a fax machine at home as well as a scanner/copier and printer, and, of course, Internet with email and a cell phone with voice mail. We have to be able to keep in touch.

Where is my Dick Tracy wrist phone? I need to save some more time.

Poetry/Joel Van Valin

The World

Beyond this bed there is a room
one of many in the house.
A house surrounded by a yard

where dogwood and lilac blossoms breathe
the night's rain. Just over the fence
in the street a man is walking home

from the bar. He stumbles a little. He sings
something—you can almost hear
the words, so still is your body.

Poetry/Lina Belar

The Future of the World

I am waiting for the day you can't buy pens anymore.
Who needs a writing instrument once telepathy replaces
　　　speech?
Already, most communication has been reduced to the
　　　fingertip.

With one swipe you can sign your name, message a friend,
capture a picture. Pens and pencils are but crutches for those
unable to see how evolution is at work.

The tap follows the thought and soon the tips of our fingers
will become the conduit for all that is glorious and beautiful
in our minds as well as the sad and forlorn.

From final tap to telepathy we will once again be able to hear
the vast symphony of the earth as it goes about its business
of living and eating and dying.

As I write this, I am watching a great blue heron poised
at water's edge, waves breaking across his bony feet
waiting for the sea to bring him the breakfast he's ordered.

Poetry/Steven R. Vogel

Small Boat

In a small boat,
the waves will come up to you close.
They will shave their chins on your fingers
and leave them white.
If you move about,
you will have them bewildered,
following, wondering how to catch up.

But if you are still,
they will speak for you—
will nudge and tip you about,
your mind lulled with you.

And when you are still,
the fish will use your shadow for a rock.
They will take your scalloped margins
for granted—
will make off with your wishes
as they flow from you.

But there are few wishes in a small boat,
no steps to take or leave,
no places to make firm,
to crowd around foundations.

There are seldom regrets,
and the breezes will make off with them—
will make eddies of the horizon,
such as it is,
its deplorable edge tempting water
to be straight,
to predict when you must nod off.

Fiction/Katie Gilbertson

The Good Son

It was time for the damn kid to get out of the house. He was going on thirty, after all. His parents were in despair that he was apparently incapable of taking care of himself, finding a wife or providing them with a grandchild.

"We need to do something," said Betty DeMars.

"Okay, what?" asked Glen, her husband of thirty-five years.

"We need to get him out of the house!"

"I know but you have to admit it's sometimes convenient for him to be around. I mean he does mow the lawn . . . "

"After you nag him for a week."

"And he lifts the heavy stuff . . . "

"If you can get him to lift himself off his fat butt first."

"He might meet a girl . . . "

"What, between the couch and the refrigerator—I doubt it."

Glen stood, perplexed. "What did you have in mind?"

Betty had it all worked out. "We're going to move and not tell him."

"Say what?"

"Well, we'll tell him but we won't tell him exactly where and we won't help him get settled somewhere else. He will have to do it himself. There will be plenty of notice and he won't want to come with us—what's a thirty-year-old kid going to do in a retirement community?"

"I guess this means you are finally serious about selling the house and the bait shop," commented Glen hopefully.

"Yes sir, I am! I'm tired of never being able to go away during the summertime and all the complaints when they don't catch any fish, like it's our fault. There hasn't been any good fishing in Lake Minnetonka for twenty years! Plus I am sick of living here above the bait shop. It smells terrible. No one ever wants to come over."

That night at dinner, Betty casually mentioned to their son Marty that they were thinking about selling the bait shop and retiring.

"Okay," he said with his mouth full.

"I know you won't be interested in following us to a retirement community, so you'll have to find another place to live."

"Cool," said Marty. "How much will you give me?"

"Give you for what?" asked Glen.

"How much will you give me every month for my own place? I can get a pretty good one-bedroom by the lake for about $1,000. Then I need to get furniture and stuff. Plus internet, Netflix and all that extra stuff. Plus spending money. I could probably make it on $3,000 a month."

Betty and Glen stared at their son, aghast. "You don't really think we are going to support you?"

"Why not? You're taking my house and my job at the bait shop. The only thing I own is my car and, by the way, the insurance is due. What am I supposed to do?"

Glen was turning red. "I expect you to pay your own insurance and find another job and rent your own apartment. You have till September 15 as long as we get a sale."

That week both the business and the home went on the market. Marty shrugged at the sight of the sign. He was slightly miffed when he had to leave for real estate showings, but he went over to his friend's house and thought about having his own place. How cool would that be? He still had no word from his parents about what they were giving him to live on. He knew that the Realtor was asking for $350,000 for the home and the business so he figured he should get about half, then a monthly payment of $3,000. He was thinking about a trip to Mexico that winter. He didn't know any girls but if he offered to pay for their trip from the $175,000 he expected, he was sure he could find a taker.

In July, a SOLD sign went up outside the bait shop. Closing was set for October 1. With great restraint, Betty and Glen refrained from saying anything to Marty about his need to provide for himself except to tell him that there would be no money forthcoming. None.

At first, Marty was steaming mad! They owed it to him. Weren't they pulling the rug out from under everything he had? It was their fault. He stayed in his room sulking. That would show them.

The summer crawled on. Betty and Glen ordered a dumpster and started tossing a lifetime of junk over the high rusted sides. Marty didn't do a thing. He figured they could not sell the house out from under him or they would come to their senses and cough up some cash.

On September 8, he went with some friends to their cabin in the Park Rapids area. He laughed when he thought of his parents' evil plans in limbo 'cause he wasn't budging. He figured when he got back on the 14th, his mom would have gotten a nice place for him and bought furniture and fixed everything up, plus filled the refrigerator with all his favorite things. That is what she had always done and Marty saw no reason for her to change now.

On the 14th, his friends dropped him off to a vacant-looking bait shop. Marty tried all the doors. They were locked. He climbed the tree beside the building and looked in the window of his bedroom. It was empty. He could not believe his eyes! His car was parked on the street. He went over to it. There was a note on the windshield:

Dear Marty: the closing got moved up so we are on our way to Florida. I put all your stuff in your car. Your bedroom furniture was in such bad shape we tossed it. The keys to your car are in the glove compartment. Let us know your new address when you get settled. You can leave a text on my cell. Love, Mom.

Marty slowly walked over to the car. The front and back seat were packed to the roof with clothes, shoes, bedding, video games and stuff he could not even identify.

It was late. He extricated a pillow from the floor of the front seat and took off down Wilshire Boulevard, looking for a new life.

Poetry/Amy C. Rea

Christmas Eve, State Highway 21

Another Christmas. Maybe the last.
Returning from assisted living,
dusk, driving to beat
the all-engulfing darkness
that gently drifts over rural roads
in an inevitable slow covering
like a blanket shaken out.
All is calm
but all will not be bright
much longer.

The slow violet spread of sunset
softens the fields of nubby tweeds, blurs
farmhouses, barns
tucked into windbreaks,
farm machinery hibernating.
No streetlights, stoplights, just
ever-deepening twilight

Then
around the bend
past the abandoned railway museum
a silo, plain, gray
but for a lighted star
perched on the domed roof
not lighting the way
but easing the dark.

Poetry/**Reprinted from Talking Stick 6, 1998*/Eric Wolff

Jason, My Humility Keeper

Spine heaven-bent
one of Jerry's kids.
Implanted back rods remain
to show past and future pain.
At twenty-one he remains a child,
a mind fostering childish hope.

Reality is weakened muscles wasting,
waiting to die.
Is that toothless smile always on?
I am shamed by his courage,
his nonstop happiness.

A blur of teen years running robbed.
Special races, ribbons, medals,
alone remain of my brother's past victories.
I am humbled by my fortunes
honored by his.
Dreams crumple and die,
like a political promise,
never to be.

From a run, a walk, to a crawl
to wheels rolling with cries of why.
No more tracks of his own.
Dusty dreams now remain
of what's to come.

Poetry/Marlene Mattila Stoehr

Night Vigil

Stillness marked the passing hours
of the year's longest night.
Nurses glided in, gently glided out
with unspoken words of shared sadness.
Silence. Only silence. Pervasive silence,
under the ever-lengthening shadow of death.

Hour by hour the bleak night passed,
and at dawn of the winter solstice, a soul,
ever at one with the rhythms of God's creation,
also relinquished darkness to journey to the Light.

The gash inflicted upon the snow-blanketed earth
that it may receive the tired body will heal in time,
as numbed hearts also will heal,
as seasons renew from solstice to solstice.

Fiction/Gail Lipe

Things Change

"Mom's sick."

"Yeah."

"She's in the hospital."

"Oh."

"Are you going to come?"

"No."

And so the conversation went with my sister, my elbow on the windowsill of my forest green Kia with my forehead in my hand.

"I don't know if she's going to make it."

"Oh."

"I would hate for the next time you see her to be at her funeral."

The motor sputtered to life as I turned the key. The familiar drone was a combination of a cat's purr and the rhythmic click of a katydid, though not as loud.

The car inched away from the apartment building where Mom has shared a one-bedroom apartment with Tibbet and Buffy since Dad died. They miss her. Tibbet, a blue-grey, strong-willed cat, has been with Mom the longest, though the little buff-colored, tiger-striped Buffy believes Mom belongs to her.

"Why don't you come to see Mom?"

"Life. Money."

"Last Christmas she offered to pay your way."

"But not my partner's."

My sister had not come home to Minnesota in many years. Nor would she meet us when we went other places. I saw her once in her home state. She backed away from me. I saw her another time. She let me stay at her house overnight when I visited my daughter.

"You could have come."

"If your husband was in the hospital would you leave him?"

"Yes, depending on the circumstances."

Her partner had many health problems—diabetes, heart issues, and more—that had plagued her for more than the ten years she and my sister were together.

"Was she in the hospital?"

"No, but she could have been."

Her partner's family became her family. She lived with her partner and her partner's ex-husband. Their children and grandchildren became my sister's children and grandchildren.

"I don't know you anymore. You know nothing about me. You know nothing about my children or grandchildren. Why?"

"It's deeper than that."

The night road disappeared into the darkness of my distraction. No matter. The car knew its way back to the hospital.

"They can't get the mucus out of Mom's lungs."

"Oh."

"They put a vest on her that fills with air and then vibrates. She looks like an alien."

"What drugs are they giving her?"

"The normal ones, plus insulin."

"What kind of insulin? I want to talk to a nurse."

It was just the two of us growing up, one dark and one light—hair, skin, eyes, everything. One coordinated and mechanical, one clumsy and a hippie without the drugs. Dad wouldn't let me behind a mower for fear I would hurt myself. That hurt her.

She had music in her soul that flowed out perfectly like a river gliding over stones heading to the power and passion of a waterfall, and then calming as it flows to the oceans of others' hearts. I loved music. It moved and refreshed me. I breathed it in but could not exhale it. I could never create new music. I envied that in her.

She perceived me popular and pretty, though I had no idea. She envied that.

We were close. I was maid of honor at her first wedding and she at mine. She is a Godparent to some of my children.

"I'm doing the best I can."

"Have the nurse call me."

"I'm up here dealing with this all the time. Why don't you want to see Mom?"

"It's deeper than that."

When she lived in Duluth, I would pack up my four children and drive four hours to spend the weekend with her. We filled her tiny one-bedroom house on the hill. Sometimes I would leave the kids at home and go alone. I loved sitting on the couch in her screened-in porch overlooking the city. Especially at night.

Once, she called me from Hinckley when she lost control while gambling. I told her to come to my house. She came. We talked. My husband had work to do the next day on one of our rental properties. We put her to work. We paid her. She had enough money to go home.

The lights loomed over the car in the hospital parking lot, their beams cutting through the cold, damp air. My skin tingled as I ambled toward the door.

"Why don't you want to know me?"

"It's deeper than that . . . I'll write."

She hasn't.

Poetry/Joni Norby

Our Last Day

11 a.m., yet it seems
an evening glow spreads
across the parlor where you lie
midnight still. Chestnut hair
falls back from your face,
blue eyes sealed under
long black lashes. A few
faint whiskers hint
at manhood.
Settled under a blanket
of soft blue cotton
I'm startled by the bed
of ice you lie upon.
I touch
the tip of your nose,
the lobe of your ear,
the pink of your mouth,
all held so dear by me.
I talk of parties and friends
and plan aloud a fitting end.
You smile at this,
I'm sure I see you smile.

Poetry/Kim A. Larson

Soiled

You sit as though helpless,
your hand reaching, holding
a glass marble, bright blue
like her angelic eyes. She
trusts you, her grandfather
on her mother's side. Yet
you lure her with trinkets,
not to give, but to take.

She fights to wash from her
your stench of Brylcreem,
cigar smoke on your breath,
your clothes, your grimy
touch that sears her like
a branding iron, embedding
your image forever.

Her marriage, short-lived,
much like her childhood
a nightmare of remembrance.
Your touch she feels as he
reaches for her, groping
the darkness for his buried
jewel. But she a mere
illusion long gone.

A handful of pills she pops,
medicating, her prescription
to numbing the pain. Trapped
by your memory, she utters
no sound, drowning in
an abyss of shame.

Poetry/Cathy Ann Wood

Descents

I came into being high above the earth
and drifted down in gentle darkness
to settle softly upon my sisters.

The wind rose with the sun and tumbled me
against a line of tall golden grasses.
With the sun's rays slanting across the field,
my sisters and I are
a sparkling mantle upon the land.

But it will not last.
The sun, commanding my circle of life, will pull me back.

Perhaps in my next life,
I will rage down in a Nor'easter along the coast,
or perhaps I'll be a raindrop in the Smoky Mountains and
          join
a stream where the delicate deer will drink.

Remember me when you catch a snowflake on your tongue.

Fiction/Charles Johnson

Beanie's First Piano Lesson

It was the sort of Saturday that every young boy feared: his first piano lesson ever. Beanie's mom dressed him in his best school clothes, put him in the car, and headed off for the piano teacher's house in the next town.

Beanie had heard of Mrs. Maarko. She was this old lady who gave piano lessons. She was also known for being the crabby lady in town who gave out the worst Halloween candy, drove her car too slowly, and had a short temper. This wasn't going to go well at all.

They pulled up in front of the house just before 10:30. They looked up at the older two-story residence, painted dark green with beige trim, innocent enough for Beanie—until he realized the house looked like a scary face: the upstairs windows seemed to scowl, vines grew over the windows, looking like bushy eyebrows, the door became a big, fat nose, and the porch gave him a nasty sneer. They got out of the car.

"Let's go. She's waiting for us." She passed through a squeaky gate that sounded as if it were from a horror movie. Beanie reluctantly made his way through the gate, joining his mother up the steps. She pushed the doorbell buzzer.

The door swung open immediately. There stood Mrs. Maarko, all six feet two inches of her.

A black dress covered her frame, draping below her knees. White socks sagged over ugly shoes. Steel-grey hair covered her head, pulled in a tight bun. She looked down at him through rimless glasses. A small black chain dangled from the bows and around her neck. Fake eyebrows had been drawn too high, giving her a look of constant surprise.

"Herbert? Yes. You will come in," she commanded. She held the door for them.

Mrs. Herbert smiled. "Thank you, Mrs. Maarko. I'm just dropping off Beanie for his piano lesson. I will be doing some shopping in town. When should I be back?" She gave Beanie a nudge. "You do your best now, Beanie."

Mrs. Maarko dismissed her with a wave of her hand. "Very well. One hour. You go now." Unceremoniously, Mrs. Herbert left.

She turned to the lad on the porch. "Master Herbert, follow me."

He entered the house as the door seemed to close all by itself with an eerie *whoosh*. Beanie found himself in the front room of the house.

"You will sit here." Mrs. Maarko pointed to an overstuffed couch near the piano. "Your mother called you Beanie. That is not your real name. Tell me what it is." She sat on the piano bench, waiting his answer.

Beanie gulped like a guppy in an aquarium. "It's Gordon, Mrs. Maarko. Gordon Ross Herbert."

"I will call you Master Gordon. You will call me Miss Udriga. Let's begin. You listen, I play." She gestured to the piano. "This is my piano, Genevieve. I named her after my aunt in Poland. I grew up there."

Mrs. Maarko swung her legs under the piano. She rubbed her hands, took a relaxing breath and began to play.

Beanie didn't expect to hear such music. He listened intently for a few minutes, but then allowed his gaze to check out the room. There were pictures on the wall, knickknacks on the shelves and even some trophies and medals. This was the room of an old lady, yes, but there was something about it that fascinated Beanie. He turned his attention back to Mrs. Maarko.

As Mrs. Maarko played on, Beanie noticed something. She seemed to shed the firm and stolid posture. As the music flowed out of the piano, she became a ballerina on the keys. Her fingers danced through the trills and arpeggios. Her body swayed with the music. Her face loosened its serious quality. Beanie decided she was no longer the scary person who answered the door just a few minutes ago.

Mrs. Maarko finished playing and turned to him. She tilted

her head as if to ask what he thought. Mesmerized, Beanie let out a breath.

"That was really something, Mrs. Maarko. Wow."

"Ah, ah . . . remember, that's Miss Udriga. Now it's your turn. Come sit on the bench, Master Gordon. Genevieve is waiting for you." She stepped away from the piano.

Her words carried enough force to move Beanie from the couch to the piano. He sat there facing the keys, not knowing what to do.

"But Mrs. Maa . . . ah, Miss Udriga, I don't know how."

Mrs. Maarko made the sound of a combined grunt and laugh. She began to teach. "You see, Master Gordon, the difference between you and me is the skill. You have the heart to play the piano just as I do. All you need is that skill. We'll start there."

His posture was first: how to sit straight and tall on the bench, how to hold his hands over the keyboard like they were gently holding tennis balls, how to stay relaxed. She led him through these steps, requiring him to stand and walk away from Genevieve and then return, sitting properly as she had instructed. She showed him how to play a C Major scale, and which fingers to use.

"And now, Master Gordon, we pause. Follow me." Mrs. Maarko led Beanie to a glass case across the room. She selected an old photo in an oval iron frame. The blue paint had worn off but a few flecks still appeared along the edges. She handed it to Beanie.

"That's my father with the cello. My mother is holding me, and that's my older brother Dieter."

Beanie studied the faces. The parents looked stern, the children polite. He turned the frame over and read out loud some handwriting on the back.

"Warsaw, Poland. 1941. Gee, Miss Udriga, that's pretty cool."

Mrs. Maarko returned the picture to the shelf, amused at his words. "Yes, Master Gordon, as you said, pretty cool. Let's go back to Genevieve."

The next part of the lesson found Beanie looking at the first pages of the lesson book. He learned about the treble clef, the staff and how time signatures worked. He knew these things from school, but somehow with Miss Udriga it was clearer, more alive. They worked on playing the first song in the book. She marked the book as his first assigned page to practice. Mrs. Maarko announced another break.

"Stay here, Master Gordon. I have something to show you." She left her chair and retrieved an item from a hook on the wall. "Read this out loud for me."

It was a wooden plaque, the size of a large book. A metal plate was attached to it on which appeared words in some language he had never seen. He had no idea how to read these kinds of letters.

"This isn't in English. I don't know what it says." Beanie returned it to Miss Udriga.

"Oh, how foolish of me. I forgot that it is in Polish. Here's what it says." She took the plaque, straightened her glasses, and read aloud. "'To Walter Maarko, Master Cellist. Ten years, Principal Cello: Warsaw Philharmonic.' That's my father. He was a very accomplished cellist." She glanced at Beanie. "It is dated as October 15, 1943. The next day we were suddenly moved by the German army to the town of Terezin." She paused in a strange way. Beanie noticed a sad look in her eyes and a bit of sorrow. He could tell from her face that this was very dear to her. Her eye caught the time on her watch. "Oh, look at the time. I will have to tell you more next time. Back to Genevieve." Beanie wanted to study the plaque some more, but she turned and placed it back on the wall.

Back at the piano, the two reviewed everything they had done so far. In the lesson book, she wrote all that he should practice. She closed the book.

"Master Gordon, that will be all for today. And now, I hear your mother coming." Mrs. Maarko escorted Beanie to the door as Mrs. Herbert climbed the stairs. Mrs. Maarko opened the door and Beanie stepped out.

"Same time next week, Master Gordon. Practice every day and think about your skills, and remember what I said about your heart."

Beanie bowed to her, which seemed like the right thing to do. "Thank you, Miss Udriga." He skipped down the porch and took his place in the front seat of the car.

His mother stayed long enough to pay Mrs. Maarko. She came to the car and asked him how the first lesson went.

"Oh, you know, Mom. It was okay."

As they pulled away, he turned back to look at Mrs. Maarko's house. He would have to remember her father's name, and that town Terezin. He knew he would be at the computer as soon as he got home—and yes, practice his piano, too.

Poetry/Mary A. Conrad

Haiku

stars cradle the dark
like stones embrace streams, and clouds
envelop the wind

Poetry/Sonja Kosler

We Are All Related

April sun peels back the last scab of winter ice.
Morning mists conceal the greening trees.
Ms. Frog calls to her Mister Right.
Turtles discover they are free.

Morning mists conceal the greening trees.
Mother earth gives a stretch and yawn.
Turtles discover they are free.
Soothing pink salve arrives with dawn.

Mother earth gives a stretch and yawn.
She gazes upon winter wounds.
Soothing pink salve arrives with dawn.
Loons paint the lake with sunset tunes.

She gazes upon winter wounds.
Healing renewal has begun.
Loons paint the lake with sunset tunes.
They remind us we are one.

Healing renewal has begun.
Ms. Frog calls to her Mister Right.
They remind us we are one.
April sun peels back the last scab of winter ice.

Poetry/Amy C. Rea

Watching the Weather in Eau Claire

Is it cold there? Will it snow?
Will the campus's giant hill
seize up, slick, in a sudden squall,
a Mt. Everest of ice?
Will my son,
novice climber,
stand at base camp
see the higher camp of
dorms above the icefall,
and wish he had
the crampons I offered,
the rope I held,
Gore-tex, balaclava, oxygen
I tried to tie to him,
before beginning his ascent
with none of it?

Poetry/David Eric Northington

A Parade in the Snow

A parade of shocked people roll past
Staring in silence at the horror
One mile of heads not looking away
Denying a simple decency to a dead man
Paramedics compress his rib cage
Failing to squeeze life back into him
Cracking bones protest the violence

A red pickup truck thrown into the ditch
Upside down like a child's discarded toy
Flashing lights police and another ambulance
One more wasted statistic that was preventable
Snow blows across the four-lane road
We voyeurs watch guilty
Thankful it wasn't us

Creative Nonfiction/René Bartlett Montgomery

Independence Day

Kenichiro, Kenichiro. His name became my mantra. I pedaled down the road, pumping in time to the chant, letting mantra morph to daydreams of Ken with his wispy black hair, dreamy smile, chocolate fondue eyes, and envious eyelashes.

Jimmy, a retired American Navy man, and his wife Yumiko lived on the outskirts of Saga. He owned an American bar, which he closed every July 4 to host a barbecue. He invited neighbors, customers, and American English teachers. When he invited me, he promised an American-sized steak and good Mexican tequila. "Make sure you come hungry," he warned.

This ride would leave me hungry, but I came to Japan hungry. At twenty-six, I was unemployed, tired of moving from job to job, of seeing couples everywhere, and of being the bridesmaid in weddings. I doubted I would find what I sought in Japan, but adventure couldn't hurt. So, I came to teach at the language school.

During my first classes, I learned I was a stale Christmas cake. At twenty-six, I thought of myself as a strong, independent, adventurous woman. My class of housewives quickly presented an alternative view. In Japan, they told me, they believed Christmas cake was fresh through the twenty-fifth, but after that, nobody wanted stale cake. Touché!

Students also introduced me to Jimmy's bar, around the corner from the school. Jimmy played American oldies. My students knew the lyrics to Johnny Cash, the Everly brothers, The Four Aces, and Elvis, thanks to Jimmy. They came for the music, to practice English, and to drink. Jimmy and I got along well. I often worked with him on Saturday nights. I served traditional Izakiya snacks, poured beer, and engaged customers in English conversation.

One night David, a fellow teacher, came in with his girlfriend, Reiko. Ken and his classmates soon joined them.

David spoke fluent Japanese and had been dating Reiko for a year. They came on the excursions Ken and his class took with me—to the noodle stand, the pottery factory in Arita, the mountainside restaurant. I imagined they would move beyond dating soon. When they left, David stood up to slip Reiko's coat on for her. In the process, he grabbed her hand and gave her a little kiss. Ken stood up to leave, winked at me and said, "See you Monday, Sensei!"

I felt no surprise when my heart and stomach fluttered. Ken seemed interested, or at least I wanted him to have interest in me but, even though I had been in Japan only five months, I knew the taboo of their men dating foreign, especially American, women. I wondered if Ken held modern enough beliefs to date an American. I wondered if I could lose the title of "sensei."

"Hey," Jimmy said as we left. "I invited Ken, Reiko, and David to the barbecue."

"That's great!" I said containing my flutters.

"Yeah, thought you'd say that." Jimmy smiled.

I arrived in time to help prepare foods. I made gyoza and yakitori. Yumiko knew these pork dumplings and Japanese chicken skewers didn't fit Jimmy's party theme, but these were her comfort foods. I shaped dumplings and I wondered about Ken's surprise.

After our last class, Ken had stayed to thank me for the lesson. A sliver of his dark hair fell across one eye and he pushed it aside as he stood to go. "I'll see you at Jimmy's party," he added. "I'm excited to join a real American celebration." He stepped out the door, and turned back to add, "Oh, I will have a surprise for you there!"

Yumiko gave my dumplings her approval. I wondered if Ken would ask me to go to Nagasaki Peace Memorial without the class. He knew I really wanted to go there. I carried the dumplings out in a beautiful pottery bowl. Yumiko bought it from the same factory I visited with Ken and the class. American Flags and banners adorned the fence posts. A few guests had steak sizzling over flames. Coolers had everything a celebration needed on ice. Fireworks were set up away from the grills. I settled into the celebration.

David and Reiko arrived, finding me by the coolers. We grabbed drinks and sat in lawn chairs. David opened Reiko's can and handed it back to her. I noticed an extra sparkle in the sunshine, as Reiko reached for it. "Hey, do you two have news?" I asked.

"Yes, you see we do!" She stretched her hand my way.

As Reiko told me about the engagement, Kenichiro arrived. Perfect timing! Hunger rumbled in my stomach. I'd ask him to grill my steak and steal time to talk with him. However, before I could get my steak, I notice the Japanese woman wearing a yukata, a bright summer kimono worn to festivals, standing with him.

"Have you met Naoko?" Reiko asked.

"No, is that his sister?" I asked, sure that she was not

"No, she is his Omiai—his arranged marriage potential."

My stomach and heart made a thud. Reiko explained that Ken's parents hired a Nakodo, a matchmaker, because Ken had reached the end of the acceptable age to marry. He didn't take his marriage opportunities seriously, so they stepped in to prevent family embarrassment. I learned this was their third meeting, and by the end of the party Ken would have his marriage agreement, or a polite refusal in which both save face. Their first meeting took place two weeks ago; everyone agreed there was potential. For the second date, Ken took her to Nagasaki Peace Memorial.

Well, that is a surprise! I thought, feeling no flutters in my heart and only hunger in my stomach. I watched Naoko offer Ken appetizers before tasting any herself. I got up and put my steak on the grill, sprinkled it with spicy seasoning, and cooked it to medium rare perfection.

Jimmy handed me a shot of good Mexican Tequila. I sliced the steak, took a bite, feeding my hunger. "Damn good steak." We raised our glasses. "Happy Independence Day, Jimmy."

Poetry/Tarah L. Wolff

Fire and Water—A Leo and a Pisces

It was across his chest in
blue ink that I read every day
when I went to sleep when I
woke or when I made love to him
I traced the ink with my fingers and
the words stayed with me
in the light of dawn they
were water over his skin which
was as red as embers
and I understood
how water and fire could be
without destroying the other
as though his body were a sea on fire
but I knew better because
it was not his body that was the sea
but mine as I was the water
and he was the fire skimming
over every last surface of
me like a red sunset across an
ocean flickering flames into every last wave
I touched those words as though they had
been written there (left there) for me
to find and taste and touch as
though one day long ago he
chose them for me
whom he did not yet know
and they had been waiting for my
lips and my tongue and my fingers
to one day finally claim and
for my ocean to slip over
the forms of him (like blue ink) cooling
the rage and sating his
flames

Poetry/Thomas C. Stetzler

Nightmare Blues
—For Rosemary

That loco black mare
gallops off in the moonlight
with your fingers knotted in her mane,
your legs tight to her flanks.

In no time stars are flying past,
night wind cooling your face,
hair streaming out behind.

Abruptly, the mare stops
tossing you off over her head.
You tumble down, down,
through the inky black air
picking up speed
closer and closer to the ground . . .

You sit up with a sudden cry.
I gather you in, hold you close
until your breathing slows.

You lie back down, close your eyes
but half an hour later you are in
the living room sitting out the night,
the mare gone off to forage
where the darkness grows.

Poetry/*Honorable Mention*/Larry Ellingson

Things Unsaid

In those long nights
when desire is too weak to give rise to passion
but strong enough to leave us restless,
the drops of things said
collect and form and flow
to the ocean of things unsaid.

My tongue was a useless flap when she first came to me
with a small smile and an open robe.

There was that veil of soft and silent snow
that fell around us and muffled all the world.

And there was that blazing day when she raised her arms
to fly on a cooling breeze while I watched, mute and dazed.

And when we crumpled in grief we each lifted the other
with a look, a touch, whispers without words, until we stood
        again.

I move to her time and she moves in my space,
but there is no time, no space
save that which is between our moving bodies.

For soon enough we will shuffle and complain
of this pain and that pain
and the revelation of wonders will cease.

So half asleep I half resolve
that when the sun comes 'round
I will take my vessel to the ocean
and I will fill it to the brim,
and I will carry it home
to shower her with praise and passion.

Poetry/Adrian S. Potter

Unsolicited Advice Received During My Wedding Reception

Sometimes it's smart to stay silent rather than win an
    argument.
You'll sleep better in your bed than on the couch. Be
    dependable,

but not boring. She has control, of course, but you do have
    influence,
if you decide to wield it. Which is to say, act like a man and
    your wife

will respect your manhood. Just be confident and she'll
    follow your lead,
during waltzes and in life. Who knows why? Women are
    like TV channels.

Eventually you have to pick just one, so choose one you
    enjoy watching.
Ignore all the other fish in the sea swimming past you.
    Please enunciate

when speaking into the microphone. Keep your own bank
    account. Hold
down a decent job. Buy her flowers, but only when it's not
    predictable.

Pray together and you'll stay together. Bad news sounds a
    bit sweeter

> > >

when it's punctuated by a kiss. Two Geminis means four
      personalities

under one roof, so beware. You're both go-getters, but
      someone still
needs to be the homemaker. Don't drink too much. Try not
      to put on

too much weight. Don't have kids too soon. If she goes on
      the pill,
her boobs will get bigger. Don't do anything that results in
      regret.

She could do better. You could do worse. Grandma
      would've loved
the ceremony if she was alive. Stand up straight or you'll
      look short

in the pictures. If you don't smile, people will think you're
      unhappy.
A happy wife makes for a happy life. Always keep the gift
      receipt.

Fiction/Niomi Rohn Phillips

Rescue

Linda was tired of the unrelenting winter. She was tired of David too, and she even surprised herself when her apathy turned to instantaneous fury.

"How could you be so insensitive? How can you understand so little about me?"

"Be reasonable, Linda," he said. "When I mentioned Easter in Hawaii, Paul picked right up on it. Said Trudy had never been to Hawaii. He'd like to take her on a vacation with us. Like us to get to know her better."

"What could you be thinking? The last time we vacationed with Paul, Joanne was alive. It's too soon. And I don't want to get to know Trudy better."

"You have to move on, Linda."

"I'm not ready to move on. That's trite. And this isn't just any vacation. We need this time alone."

She replayed the scene in her head for days, nursing her grudges, gathering grievances from forever like a dead bouquet.

David cajoled her with a litany of advantages—the car rental would be cut in half, they could share the driving . . . and the cooking. She didn't care about saving money on car rental. And she didn't want to share the cooking. She didn't want to be *the cook* either. Trudy obviously didn't like to cook. Trudy and Paul ate out twice a week on "date nights."

Paul and his first wife had been their friends for decades. Their kids grew up together. Their first grandsons were born within days of each other. Linda had nothing in common with the new wife. Trudy was fifteen years younger. She didn't have kids or grandkids. She read romance novels.

Snow, wind, cold, togetherness, had distilled David and Linda's differences this winter. Everything David did annoyed her, including packing for this trip. She started with a list. Then she tucked her shoes into bags, made tidy rolls of bathing suits and shorts, slipped dresses in plastic bags to prevent wrinkles. She packed with smugness, congratulating herself on having at least learned never to share a suitcase with David. He piled his shorts, shirts, and underwear on the bed, opened his duffel bag, tossed everything in, and zipped it.

"That's a mess," she said, for the hundredth time in as many trips.

And he responded as always, "It fits doesn't it? The TSA guys rummage in it anyway."

They needed a new script.

The scenery on the drive to the airport was the perfect backdrop to Linda's mood. Dried grass in ditches, leafless trees, and shades of brown met the cloudy gray sky to the horizon. Tractors, like desolate sculptures, were poised to move onto the plowed brown fields *if* spring ever came.

Her anger with David festered between naps on the eight-hour flight from Minneapolis to Kaua'i Island with Paul and Trudy cuddling across the aisle. But her anger slipped away unwittingly with the summer-like breeze on the road from the airport to the beach house.

Blue, blue-green ocean reached to the blue sky, and frosted waves washed the shore on one side of the winding coastal highway. Towering mountains in crenelated shades of lush green climbed to the sky on the other.

Then the beach house—palms, pink hibiscus, and purple Bougainvillea in the front yard facing the street; in the backyard—ocean—fifty yards from the lanai to the shore; and a view of the mountains from every room including the kitchen.

A trip to the grocery store was the first group occasion. A cluster. They should have planned menus as Linda suggested. David pushed the cart and they tossed things in the basket, suggesting meals. "Fish tonight?" "How about grilling steak?" "Do you eat blue cheese?" "Red wine or white?"

The commotion, blocking the aisles, trying to decide what to buy, embarrassed Linda.

Paul suggested Spam. "President Obama eats Spam," he said.

"No way. I'm not eating that crap." David's voice carried a mile. And he was conspicuous in his suede Merrells with his black socks. He didn't care if everyone else wore sandals. He had never worn sandals. He never would wear sandals.

The morning shopping experience stifled Linda's pleasure in the place, and her enthusiasm waned when high winds and torrents of rain came through the island. Surf warnings and flash floods. They were stuck inside.

Next day the sun came out, and so did the tourists—not the wind-your-way-between beach mats of Waikiki, but close. Pickups full of boogie boards and surfboards were parked next to the pier. Little people raced into the ocean, screaming with delight as gentle waves washed over them. Beach umbrellas sprouted like colorful mushrooms everywhere. Congregations were setting up canopies, arranging toys and coolers for the day. Couples strolled along the shore, holding hands. Joggers swished by.

David insisted on walking down the beach to get away from the crowds. Linda tried to deter him. "Doesn't look like there are any surfers, either tourists or locals, on the other end of the beach. Maybe it isn't smart to wander so far from the crowd."

The surf was six to eight feet high where they were headed, roiling, foamy white, unlike the quiet rhythmic breakers of the inner bay. David strode ahead carrying a boogie board. Paul and Trudy followed, her bronzed, long-legged body in a wisp of a white bikini. She apparently had never read the research about tanning beds. Linda straggled behind, conscious of the zinc oxide on her nose.

Only three days and Linda had her fill of Paul's fawning and Trudy's *Can I get you a gin and tonic, honey* devotion.

"Paul adores Trudy," a friend had recently remarked.

Linda had repeated it to David with sarcasm and more than a tinge of envy. It was a long time since she'd been adored, if ever. She wasn't the type to be adored . . . but it might be nice for a change.

Only three days and Linda was even tired of herself. "I'm going to get some exercise," she announced. As she turned and walked away, she noticed a stanchion with red icons of waves and a swimmer—WARNING DANGEROUS SHORE BREAK.

She picked up the pace. Her feet sank into the sand. Then she strolled, gazing beyond the crowded beach to the ocean. The blue-green water met the sky in the cup-like bay, protected by the lush, green mountains rising into fluffy clouds on the west. The rhythmic splash of waves accompanied the happy activity on the shore. She remembered writer Anne Lamott's *Three Essential Prayers—help, thanks, wow.* This was Thanks and Wow.

Near the pavilion, a bearded man in a white robe, book in hand, stood facing a young man in pink shorts with pink plaid shirt, his partner in tan and blue. Both were adorned with plumeria lei. A wedding. Linda smiled inside and out. Calmed and content, she walked the mile to the pier and turned back.

She heard a bull horn. "COME IN! COME IN!" Then sirens. She stopped and watched a red and white truck, with bright yellow boogie boards on the rack, race down the beach, two lifeguards in blaze-orange swim trunks, hanging onto the box. She kept walking, noticed people getting up from beach chairs, shading their eyes to see, some with binoculars. "What's happening?" she said.

"Couple of tourists got out too far."

When she got close enough to recognize Trudy standing on shore, she could also see two lifeguards on boogie boards. They were on the top of waves, then beneath the waves, the surf tossing them like toys in a foaming fury. Paul and David were black dots in the distance.

"They got out too far," Trudy said.

"I told David. I reminded him he'd never done this before.

The ocean isn't a Minnesota lake," Linda said.

Trudy put her arm around Linda. They stood together scanning the churning ocean. A second red and white truck arrived. Two more lifeguards threw surfboards into the water, flung themselves on, and paddled, fighting the surf. Blue sky. Brilliant sun. Rhythmic roar of waves. Time stopped. Linda took deep yoga breaths. *HELP.*

People congregated in spontaneous groups as word of drama and disaster spread. Forty minutes. A lone albatross swept low. Quiet mutterings of sympathy from women. Disdain from men. "Idiots . . . Stupid . . . Some tourists pay no attention to the warnings."

"Lifeguards coming in," someone shouted.

A lifeguard pushed Paul onto the shore. Paul rolled off his boogie board and stumbled out of the water. Trudy rushed to meet him.

Two lifeguards paddled in on a wave, David prone on a board between them. The crowd's silence was like one big held breath. Was he alive? Then David rolled off the board and crawled up onto the sand. He sat down, his back to them, facing the ocean. He put his head in his hands. Linda sat down and put her arms around him. No script.

Poetry/Mary Jones

Art on the Move

I'm already running late when
I have to stop for a freight train.
I'm in no mood to be entertained,
yet the graffiti rushing by on
the plain brown boxcars
dazzles me.

Oddly shaped letters and designs,
pulsing with energy,
brilliant blues, vibrant pinks, neon greens,
always outlined in black,
simple messages,
some profane, some silly.

I picture the artists, under cover of
night, sneaking around railroad yards
in some distant city
carrying spray cans of paint.
Maybe they wear ski-masks and carry
flashlights. Maybe one of them
keeps a look-out for police.

I suppose this is a crime, but I would
not arrest them. I might even hold
the flashlight.

Poetry/Rebecca Ramsden

Silver Clasp

The solid silver case fits in the palm,
a slim rounded disc, edges tapered,
the back smooth as river stone.
A skilled hand etched the cover with

fine features; a Chinese village
braced to a steep mountainside,
the fortress wall holds back the
ocean's breaking burden. Out at sea,

two boats—lone sails billow home.
Above a flock of wings fans a perfect
circle where scrolled initials—
FS—float in a full moon.

Inside the bottom half, frail silk
rests, edges a bit frayed. Once it
held the powder, now a film of
mottled beige with peach undertones,

companion puff long gone.
The top half continues to mirror.
I imagine all the times my mother
held up her face, relieved the war

was over, her love returned safely,
his naval dress blues shouldering
their promise. What visions
colored her cheeks, her wavy dark

> > >

hair framing deep brown eyes
building their life together.
Each day the compact closes,
two halves join with a snap
each day held by a silver clasp.

Poetry/Dawn Loeffler

Tomorrow's Tomorrow

The shadow of your face
lit my hazy recognition
soft, smooth lips
jagged scruff
twinkles glinting off the rising sun
through slit chocolate curtains
you slide
so large
into my existence
enveloping me into goodbyes
"love you babe"
whispered soft against my hair
muscles uplift my pain
cradling the fear
momentarily
I blink
I blink
to the day

Poetry/Larry Schug

The Anniversary Gift

Yolanda picks the green ferns in the bouquet
you give your wife on your anniversary.
When she was younger,
Yolanda could pick four hundred bundles a day,
but now her back is so sore from bending for hours,
a good day is less than half of that;
her hands are so swollen she can't work some days,
her fingers ache so that she can't sleep at night,
and that's not to mention the snakes
that sneak into the warm, humid fernery,
sprayed with the same chemicals sprayed on the ferns,
causing rashes on Yolanda's skin, which never cease to itch.
She has no protective gear and no one cares.
Yolanda is replaceable.

But you love your wife. It's your anniversary.
You hope the bouquet you bring home after work
will be enough to keep your wife from replacing you,
though if either of you knew about Yolanda,
you might opt for chocolates and wine,
but what about Miguel and his family in the vineyards,
right here in California's wine country,
eating their lunch in the backwash of sprayed pesticides.
What about his back, his hands, his ragged breathing,
what they put themselves through so they all can eat.

What about Drissa, a child slave on the cacao plantation
in the Ivory Coast or Mombi Bakayoko in Mali,

> > >

children, kidnapped for slave labor at age seven,
the beatings and malnourishment that goes into chocolate
they've never even tasted and never will.

Better to wrap your wife in your arms so tightly
that she melts like chocolate in the sun of your embrace,
kiss her like you're newlyweds on honeymoon,
tell her that her lips taste like a fine cabernet.
Write her a poem with words like roses
grown in your own garden.

Poetry/Cheryl Weibye Wilke

Farm Girl

You spoke of their butchering. The chickens—
how they fought like hell attempting to peck
and scratch your eyes out as you flashed
the red ax through their necks. So unlike, you said,
the goose, who looked at the block and laid
her head down exposing her neck just so
that you could not do it.

Fiction/Jerry Mevissen

Your Heart's Desire

Julia Roberts leaned back in the lilac leather chair, crossed her legs, and dangled a strapped pump from her painted toes. She raised her fingers to her chin in a prayer position and smiled her global-warming smile.

"This is your final question on *Your Heart's Desire*, the Celebrity Quiz Show," the announcer said. "If you answer correctly, you win anything your heart desires. Miss Roberts, are you ready?"

Julia swept the audience with a slow glance of chocolate brown eyes and nodded to the announcer. "I'm ready."

The announcer sat upright, raised his glasses on his nose, and cleared his throat. The audience sat still, spellbound. "Name five American winners of the Nobel Peace Prize."

Julia leaned forward and flashed a knowing smile. She held the audience in a suspenseful, dramatic pause. "Theodore Roosevelt, Woodrow Wilson, the American Red Cross, and Jimmy Carter," she answered. "And Martin Luther King."

The audience erupted. The announcer double-checked the answer list. Julia leaned back and smiled.

"Correct," screamed the announcer. "You've won *Your Heart's Desire*. And Julia Roberts, what is your heart's desire?"

Julia paused again, playing with the audience and the announcer. Her lips parted in a smile that rivaled the Grand Canyon. "I want to spend a weekend on Maui with Jerry . . . something, the author of *Good Shepherd*."

The silence in the auditorium was deafening. The announcer cocked his head in a quizzical pose. Julia smiled.

When I came into the house after chores, the incoming call light on the telephone blinked. Fourteen calls. I washed garden dirt from my hands, rinsed mosquito spray from my face, and brushed hay chaff from my hair. The telephone rang.

"Have you been watching television?" an unidentified voice asked.

"No," I answered. "I don't watch television. I don't own a television."

"Well, if you don't watch television, what do you do?"

"Get to the point," I said. "Another World Trade Center bombing? Another pandemic? Another assassination?"

"Nope. Better than that."

The phone call came the next morning from the publicist of *Your Heart's Desire.* Had I heard of the show? *Yes.* Was I familiar with the format? *Yes, vaguely.* Had I heard the results of the Julia Roberts episode? *Yes, from neighbors, friends, family, coworkers, high school classmates, total strangers.* Was I available the week of September 15 for a trip to Maui? I hesitated. "Let me check my calendar." I placed the phone on the counter for a respectable interval. "I think I can make that work."

We met at the Premier Club at Maui's Kahului Airport. She sat by the window beside a bouquet of orchids. The tails of her white blouse were tied in a casual knot, revealing a buttery tanned stomach. Her hair fell like fresh-cut clover across her shoulders. She wore small oval glasses and smiled as she read my book *Good Shepherd.*

"Julia," I said, steadying myself against a lamp table.

"Jerry," she said. She stood, almost to my height, and smiled. The room lit up, like it had been struck by lightning.

We rode to the Grand Wailea in her limo, talking about the book. *What prompted it? Were the characters real? Who owned the rights?*

"I'm flattered by your interest," I said, "but what are you leading up to?"

"I'd like to try my hand at directing," she said. "And I'd like to direct a movie based on your book. I want to play a role too, maybe have you create a character for me."

I pursed my lips and stared at passing palm trees. "I could

do that."

"And I'd like Bob Duval to play one of the Good Shepherd residents. Might have to flesh out his character, but I'll bet you could do that too."

That moment I could re-write *Gone with the Wind*. "I have a few short stories inspired by those characters," I said.

"Great." She grinned. "We'll talk about that."

We checked into the hotel, she conquering the lobby with a long-legged stride and a smile behind rose-colored sunglasses. I followed, feeling very Minnesotan in my Hawaiian shirt, white painter pants, and Jesus sandals.

"Meet me at the gate to the beach at nine," she said.

What felt like days later, nine o'clock arrived. Eyes closed, I stood before a full-length mirror—new swim trunks, beach towel thrown casually over a shoulder, twirling un-needed sunglasses. Bougainvillea and birds of paradise scented the lanai. Guitars strummed from behind stuccoed garden walls. Coconut oil and lime juice and fresh grated ginger flavored the sea air.

I looked in the mirror. God. My body was as white as a hospital patient's. My skinny legs belonged to a stork. My hair was frizzy from humidity. I guzzled a glass of Merlot. Then another. "What am I worried about?" I said to my fortified self. "She was married to Lyle Lovett."

We met at the beach and talked until midnight about her movies, the twins, her ranch in Taos, her directorial debut. She asked about my life, where I had been and where I was going. The hours flew.

The moon peeked over the horizon, and waves of the wide Pacific lapping on the shore fractured the moon's reflection. We shared a bottle of Merlot. Guitars strummed in the distance.

"Wanna play From Here to Eternity?" I asked.

Julia laughed. The moon reflected off a perfect set of gleaming teeth. "What's that?"

"Did you see the movie?" I asked. "Deborah Kerr and Burt

Lancaster in the beach scene? Right here on the Islands."

"Refresh my memory," she said.

I leaned on one elbow in the sand. "The moon is shining," I said in a low sexy register. "Deborah and Burt are lying on the beach. They kiss, and the waves wash up the shore and douse them. Deborah shivers, and we don't know if it's the cold water or the hot kiss."

"Wait a minute." She smiled. "Didn't we agree this would be a business relationship?"

I gritted my teeth. "Agreed, but I don't do platonic very well." I traced her smile with my fingers, a journey that took minutes. She closed her eyes. I kissed her with a gentleness that surprised me.

She leaned back and stared at the rolling surf. Flecks of moonlight danced in her eyes. A trace of mischief tickled her smile. She lifted the Merlot and drained the final drops, then relaxed on the beach towel. "You're from Minnesota, right?"

I nodded.

"Well, that's a first." She reached for my arms. "All right," she teased. "Let's see where it takes us. To the book. To the movie. Or to your heart's desire."

Poetry/ Audrey Kletscher Helbling

Confessions in a Grocery Store Parking Lot

"I have a lady friend," he confides, voice lowered
for fear others will overhear his confession
in the grocery store parking lot.
I lean toward my widower friend leaning into his cane.
"She sends me cards in the mail."
He sneaks a guilty look, awaits judgment
of the secret released to a March wind
that nips ears, clips conversations.

"What's wrong with that?" I offer,
wind wrapping words like a gift
dropped at his unsteady feet.
He hesitates, shifts his weight. Uncertainty lingers.
"She was in our wedding."
His and Nancy's, the wife whose kidneys failed,
the wife he tended for two years because
there would be no nursing home for his darling.

He's a good man, a retired painter, a musician.
He painted my living room ceiling once,
dropped by in his Buick with a bag of sun-warm sweetcorn.
Across town at the nursing home,
he squeezes out waltzes and polkas on his accordion.
Nancy resented his music, he tells me,
then pauses, silent, as if he's betrayed the dead
with an admission of marital discord.

Poetry/Marie Zhuikov

Universal Ticket

The dark man
on the street corner
taps the laminated nametag
dangling from his neck
and beckons us.

"I'm going to have to
give you a ticket,"
he says to you,
my dark man.
At our raised eyebrows and
clenched fists
he says,
"You are not holding
the lady's hand."

"I don't think
her husband would like that,"
you say.

This is the second time
a stranger has tried
to punish us
for not being together.
There was the woman
at the festival
over twenty years ago . . .

What is it?
Can they see my face shining?
Feel the low hum
of our bodies?

Since that first parting—
me on a boat,
you on a dock,
it seems the
universe
is trying to
make us answer for
something
that will take a
lifetime
to explain.

Poetry/Laura L. Hansen

Passerine; or a Bird of Open Country

You flew into my heart
like a swallow to a barn
heading straight for the loftiest place
bringing your friends
and swarming the rafters
all those wings rising and falling
at once and in syncopation
knocked my heartbeat askew
it rocked and tumbled
and a strange light breeze
whispered there
a voice I'd never heard before
and I decided to place
a small birdhouse
in the corner of my heart
and invite you in
demanding that your friends
all that bustle and noise
stay outside
but you weren't the same
without the crowd you came with
you said the birdhouse was a cage
and so I pulled the big red doors
open and left you
to huddle in the rafters
with angry eyes
or to fly

Poetry/Ryan M. Neely

I Love the Idea of You More than I Love Myself

Maggots worm their way through the corpse of our love
Gnawing, gnashing, biting, like words we used to cut each
      other
"I hate you," meant "I love you," in our twisted language
And making love was more like making war
Two bodies railing against each other, vying for control

Black and blue were the colors we wore, splashed with a
      tinge of red
We tried anything to keep from facing the truth that our love
      was dead
You brought handcuffs and silk to the bedroom, and I
      brought him
Bound and gagged by shame and fear, I helped you think I
      enjoyed it
I died that night, between your bodies, when you spent
      more time with him

Poetry/Shelley Getten

Walk
—in memory of Ellen Moore Anderson
after *Turn Right, Good Moon* (used with permission)

A sweet scent
precedes winter's
bitter chill.

Not an earthy aroma
of spring, but no less enticing.

Leaves, in the course
of breaking down—
a rich perfume.

I've wondered how it tasted
the ground paste you were given
in your final days.

What smell of oils
tenderly rubbed on your skin?

Did you wander
on your favored path
along a rocky shore
bordering
two worlds?

The one in which
your concern is always
for others—

The one in which
you join a million fallen leaves
on yet another North Shore trail
you had a hand in blazing.

Poetry/Lina Belar

Watching the Anhinga Bird in Sarasota

For two hours every day that I am here
the anhinga perches on the seawall above the bay
turning this way and that until
he's found the perfect angle of sun,
swivels his long neck to check
that no one is watching.
What is this? He's vain?
Neck of a snake. Body gone south like a pear.
He unfolds wings like a bat.
Beneath his dull dark wrapper
lurk white feathers like ivory
stolen from Africa, hidden from poachers.
He shows these treasures to no one
but the sea.

Creative Nonfiction/*Honorable Mention*/Cheyenne Marco

Breakables

The sun angles down over the lake. Light glances off the surface. The water looks like glass, sparkles like crystal. I walk down the dock with my book in my hand, looking for peace. It's so hard to find these days. I don't find it on the dock. Not today. Not when you walk down the neighbor's dock. You move with force, with purpose like everything will give way.

I keep my eyes on my book, locked down on the lines of *Jane Eyre*. My sunglasses feel like camouflage, my earbuds like an escape. I don't have to look up. I don't have to say anything. I don't give any sign that I know you're there. But of course I know. Ever since you kissed me, every cell in my body knows when you're close. Ever since I felt the weight of your body move over mine, I can't help but notice the way it moves down the stairs, over the wood planks. Ever since you left me, I am aware of the space between this dock and the one ten feet away.

You pick up a rock and throw it my way. It splashes in front of me. Droplets of water revolting against gravity, crying upward. The movement startles me and shatters my ploy. I have to look up. The playful smile you have aimed at me hits closer than the stone. Broad lips on a scruffy face. Dark eyes under heavy brows.

I try to smile. "Not even close," I say. And I look away. I have to look away or you'll see it. You'll see how much I miss being scrunched up on my couch with you just listening to Wade Bowen, how you would comfort me as I babbled about grad school, how I would hold your hand while you would tell me about how your ex-wife taunts you with pictures of the life you don't lead any more.

It always seemed like a long shot. Ten years stood between us. Your failed marriage; your inability to let it go. My refusal to take chances, to let any part of me out of my control. I was young. You were broken. Both of us more fragile than glass. But that night in April, you came to my place. My thesis defense was coming. I was grading papers. I was trying to figure out the next four years of my life. I was falling apart and needed a friend. The pizza made our stomachs hurt. The TV was small but captivating. You made me smile, when the thought of a smile seemed so far away. The TV lost its hold, and you kissed me. You held me. You threw a piece of yourself at me. And I was too blind to see it wasn't a boulder or even a stone—just a pebble. A small piece, easily thrown away.

But even the smallest pebble can crack a windshield. It doesn't take a boulder to shatter a vase.

Another rock comes sailing across the water. So small that all I can see is a gray blur. It plinks against the metal dock post a few inches from my face. I jump back. My heart beats faster. The rush is painful. I bite my tongue. The pebble tumbles to the water, breaking the surface. The ripples expand, stretching farther than they should. I smile less. Wade Bowen's songs aren't as sweet. I don't eat pizza. Damn ripples. I look closer. It's funny how they look like cracks, except bursting outward from the seams instead of caving in. A thick spider web of moving water.

That rock hits a lake bottom I can't see. It was so small but so powerful. So close.

When my youngest brother was three, some deviant found a pebble in the Hobby Lobby parking lot and slipped it into his hand without my parents' knowing. He let the thing fly in the picture frame section. The glass shelves shattered. The frames fell to the floor. I remember the lecture we all got afterward. You don't throw rocks, especially around breakables. Don't ever— ever—throw rocks.

Clearly, no one told you. Don't throw rocks, Leonard. That's how you break things.

Poetry/Susan McMillan

Broken

The pit of the heart is liquid
thick and unclear.
It does not flow
      but sags, seeps,
and despite what some may think,
      never thaws or freezes.

The pit of the heart
weighs heavy
      pushes down atop
      the tender gut—
a fist of lead, a gob
of dread clotted awkward and low—

      leaving one unable to swallow
      or let go.

Poetry/Jennifer Jesseph

Marigolds

My deck brims
with all their gold.
How they petal
their brightness
for us. I long for their color
all winter.

Even their stink fills
me with summer.

Let me live
as they do—
for months and months
of bold orange.
Let me keep their glow,
their gold, shiny awe.

When I must die
shroud me in all the marigold
yellow, orange, gold petals
like confetti
all over me, singing out.

Poetry/Kari E. Hagstrom

Tonight I Took to Bed With Me

Tonight I took to bed
with me a wizard,
a hobbit, twelve dwarfs,
a poet, a pack of werewolves
and a coyote, a couple of cats,
a snoring dog, an old dog,
and a smiling dog,
a nearly full moon,
a pearlescent overcast
dark turquoise sky,
and the white whiteness
of new-fallen
April snow coating
black gnarly oak
branches, giving them
vivid brightness.

It is a night of light,
a night of cavorting
in dreams.

Poetry/Janice Larson Braun

Family Dynamics

Of all the seven sisters,
That Monday is the strict one.
She knows that Saturday and Sunday
And even Friday, if we are being honest,
Are pretty soft.
They encourage sloth in all its forms—
Sleeping late,
Eating oneself sick on Cheetos,
And lying on the couch
To watch hours of mindless television.
Tuesday, Wednesday and Thursday,
Born followers,
Passively do whatever they're told,
So Monday is stuck
Being the disciplinarian.

By the time she stands
At the front door,
Hands on hips,
Eyes in "I see you" mode,
Saturday and Sunday
Have slipped off for a nap,
And Friday, already distracted,
Hums to herself
As she practices
Some complicated dance step.

Tuesday-Wednesday-Thursday
Stand at attention
And watch as Monday
Points imperiously,
And we,
Heads bowed,
Shoulders drooping,
Plod out the door
And down the stairs
To face the week ahead.

*Fiction/*Reprinted from Talking Stick 11, 2002/*Cynthia Ekren

Healing Choices

Watching the light move across the bleached ceiling filled my hours—calming, soothing. To lie motionless, to not think about anything at all, except the light.

The smell took on a shape, a color of whiteness and fluttering wings. It took on a sound of singing and steady heartbeats. The winged-creatures moved close and away like Mother. Birds. Angels.

God put on his blue gloves to rearrange bone and muscle. God opened the dark, hidden places and cleaned, dripped clear, healing liquid into the veins to take away the stains of violence. I looked around through a blur . . . and knew heaven.

The nurses and doctors came around often. With time, they seemed less holy, less like residents of heaven. Aware of their poking, their pleas for me to respond, I chose to remain quiet. It didn't seem at all crazy not to wiggle a toe or nod yes and no to their questions. It felt like a choice.

They called my name, "Lisl, Lisl," and asked me questions. I'd think for a moment about these questions. Where was I? In heaven? In the hospital? It felt peaceful enough, so maybe I was in heaven; that's where I wanted to be. What had happened? Had I been killed? Had someone tried to kill me?

My thinking paused, returning to the traveling light above me. Thoughts like bubbles, forming and floating up until I'd lose sight of the ones that popped or disappeared. The thoughts of what had happened were bubbles that never got past the syrupy soap stage. They were too heavy to watch. I slept.

The mind, they say, protects itself from insanity. Mine closed off and let time heal. The nurses lifted me out of bed and placed my feet on the floor. One pushed from behind, one pulled on my arms. I let them manipulate my body. With every step, I felt the buoyancy of their smiles, their hope for me. I smiled back.

"Lisl, won't you please communicate with us?"

I began to identify my caregivers. Two of the nurses seemed to be present more than the others. They told me their names—Anna and Stephanie. Both were near my age, mid-twenties; both had brown hair and brown eyes. Anna scolded herself constantly for forgetting or misplacing things. Stephanie had an air of confidence, and I believed she channeled God's power of healing. When she touched my skin, heat would radiate, the energy of her flowing through me as though I'd touched a low voltage outlet.

I uttered my first sentence in response to Stephanie's question, "Where does it hurt?" The sounds of my words had a primitive roundness to them, reduced from the utterances of vowels or consonants, identifiable letters deftly articulated. "Owwwgh." I knew the words I wanted to say. My face hurt. I spelled out the letters in my mind, F-A-C-E, and tried to say it again. "Owwgh." My hand, like a lost explorer, navigated the maze of the crisp sheet, finally finding its way out, slowly rising toward my mouth, my cheeks, my forehead. My own skin felt distant, remote. How could my face hurt, if I couldn't feel it?

Tears of confusion filled the corners of my eyes, their trickle warm, increasing my confusion. "Owgh," I tried one more time. The sunlight had reached the TV, washing out the picture.

"Do you know who did this to you?" I opened my eyes to an unfamiliar face, a woman with angelic blonde hair, translucent blue eyes. "Lisl, can you understand what I'm asking you? Did you see his face?" Why, I wondered, would this angel of God's need to ask me questions? Angels didn't speak; they only sang. Surely God could tell her about faces; she didn't need me.

The words stuck inside my mouth, peanut butter just beyond the reach of a tired tongue.

"If I showed you pictures, would you recognize him?" Her brow had three perfect lines across it. I named the lines Father,

Son, and Holy Spirit—and watched them move up and down, parallel deities.

She held out large photographs of men. One after another she held them up for me. I looked for something familiar, something to please her, to make this Holy Trinity seem less concerned. If God could watch out for me, I could help this woman.

My father, my brother, my neighbor, two old boyfriends. Their names sang in my head. Everyone familiar. Why hadn't they been to see me? Where had they been all this time?

"Can't you take that thing out of her mouth?" the angel asked Anna. She sounded angry. "How can she talk with all that wire?"

"That wire is holding her jaw together," Anna said, her voice matching the angel's in tone.

"Lisl, just lift your hand if you see a picture of the man who did this to you," the woman said. Her eyes focused hard on my right hand and she went through all the pictures again. Some of them I'd never seen before. Men looking out at me with hatred, fear, disinterest. Then my father . . . my brother, Alexander . . . my neighbor, Rudy . . . two boyfriends, Jack who liked to go bowling (Lord love him, but I hated bowling), and . . . but the second name came up blank. His face, the bright eyes, lopsided mouth, a mole next to his nose that I suggested he have removed. We had dated for one year. Exactly one year. April to April. It was my cardinal rule. If that gut feeling of knowing I'd found true love hadn't struck within a year, I moved on. Why didn't his name come to me? I lifted up my hand to take his picture from the woman.

She nodded her head; her expression seemed to be saying, "I knew it."

My parents and Alexander came to visit some time after the angel left. "Do you remember what happened, sweetheart?" Mommy asked. She gently stroked my hair as though I were still a child, the sensation on my scalp like gentle pin pricks. Nerve endings waking up.

"Na." I could get more sounds out through the metal and wires holding my face together.

"What has anyone told you?" This made me smile, like you did in a dentist chair while the hygienist made small talk, asking trivial questions you couldn't possibly answer with her hands inside your mouth. What had I heard? Attacked, unknown person. Left for dead. Miracle. A miracle. Week in and out of a coma. Healing.

"They found you out in the country. Do you know how you got there?"

My brother, Alexander, sat in the turquoise chair by the window watching the light play across the wall. I watched it with him.

"Honey? Lisl? Did you hear me?" Mommy took my hand and patted it. "Can you concentrate on my voice?"

After a while, I heard other words and understood that they thought I had brain damage. They suggested to each other I might need to stay in a nursing home for a while. Might need some counseling. They never said crazy, but I heard crazy. As in, why shouldn't she be crazy, after all she's been through?

Then one night, lying in the twilight of streetlamps shining in the window, I tried. Really tried to think about it, to see if I could remember. Like putting a toe into the cold lake first, I tested my memory. I'd been at home and heard a noise. At home, my one-bedroom house near the college campus. The house felt welcoming, a fire in the small fireplace, my plants hiding the darkness of night with their lively greenery, the dinner table I'd set. There were two place settings.

I didn't want to leave the warmth of the fire, standing in the bare-footedness of my thoughts, warming my hands. It could stop right there, without ever going any deeper. I rested until I heard the door open. If the face were familiar, would I know what it meant or would I have to go further still?

The choice came; I didn't look. I left the house, left the fire, returned to the light, the wonderful light coming from the parking lot.

Eventually the wires and metal came out of my mouth and jaw. They left the metal plate to hold my skull together and keep my eye socket from sagging. It would be there the rest of my life.

Alexander brought me home. They'd cleaned up the mess we made, I thought.

Alexander stopped me from rushing out the door, not hard to do when you need a cane to walk steadily. "You're remembering?" he asked.

"No," and I meant it. "Things seem to be tidied up in here." Turning back, it lifted, the heavy fog of knowing. The sun shone inside, illuminating shadows. My plants were lush and green.

Alexander is two years older than I am. Never married, a perennial dater. He stayed on the sofa for a solid week until he could honestly reassure my parents, who had returned to their retirement home in Florida, that I could care for myself.

"Did Ray do it?" Alexander asked as he put the last of his things in a bag. "You told the police that Ray did it."

Ray! His name was Ray. It once took me an entire summer to recall the names of all the Walton girls from *The Walton Family* TV show. I said them to myself to make sure I hadn't lost them again: Elizabeth, Mary Ellen, and Erin.

Ray.

"He's out on bail. They're still collecting evidence against him. Did you know he has a record? All assault charges."

"Ray?"

Alexander nodded. "If he comes around, you call me. Call 911."

After he left, I let it piece together, tried to imagine the night. Who came in the door? Looking at the door, I tried to picture it opening. I could see the handle moving, but there was no one there. I sat at the table, tried to see who sat across from me. No one. I tried to see the struggle, to see who picked up the iron from the fireplace and smashed my face. But there was no face. No one there.

Let it be Ray then, I thought. Like watching TV, I imagined Ray at the door, imagined him at the table, imagined the fight. In my fantasy, I gave him a black eye and a deep enough bite on his hand to require stitches. Why else would my teeth still feel a little loose? I had made a choice. Right or wrong. Crazy or sane.

I testified that Ray had attacked me. The defense attorney looked like he could chew up my fantasy and spit it back at me. But he didn't. When I said I'd hit him pretty hard in the eye and made him stumble, said I drew blood when I bit his hand, the attorney had no further questions. The prosecutor showed the jury medical records.

Ray had gotten stitches that night for a dog bite, he said.

Maybe what we think is true becomes true, our choices changing everything. I've wondered sometimes, if I'd really chosen heaven to open up my eyes to, if I'd chosen angels instead of nurses . . . God instead of the rubber-gloved doctor . . . how different would everything be.

Poetry/Charmaine Pappas Donovan

The Red Fox

At dusk I curve my way home
along Riverside Drive,
tree-lined road twisting along
the east bank of our Mississippi.
I drive slow as my eyes scan
for a red fox scampering up the steep bank
to Ahrens' Hill across the road.

This fox reminds me of the stoles
my great-aunts used to wear
when they got all dolled up
for a date or formal dinner.
Usually it took more than one fox
biting its tail to bring the fur
around Aunt Margaret's shoulders.

When she wasn't looking
I stroked the fluffy fur,
careful not to look into the gleam
of dark eyes embedded in that foxy face.
Even without teeth, I saw his wildness.
Had I thought my palm's friction
could spark him back to life?

Poetry/Romayne Kilde

The Red Sweater

On a mid-August day
with temps approaching ninety
the Salvation Army Thrift Store
comes bearing gifts for
the ladies in psych lock-up

bags and bags of clothes
are dumped precariously
on the day-room tables
a menagerie of sizes and textures
a big messy blob of colors
a crazy rainbow of smells
some musty others perfumey

the other ladies and I
with nothing else to do
except play bingo
start sorting and searching
for garments to claim as our own
my eye catches a red sweater
with black fur trim
quite luxurious and sleek
I give it a home

Many years later
I wear the red sweater, this odd souvenir
to the Como Zoo Conservatory
Holiday Flower Show
like a red badge of courage
it's a bitter reminder of those days
in the ladies lock-up psych ward

Poetry/Ryan W. Keller

Crowns and Rebels

Rebels don't dream of crowns.
Crowns dream of victorious rebels.
Rebels only dream of freedom.
Crowns hope to be stolen
from bloody and rolling heads.

Crowns care not of struggles
once endured by the sweaty brows
upon which they now rest.
They care about the sun
being upon their golden backs.

Lengthy shadows occupy thoughts
and feed the unbridled desires.
Stand tall and cast long,
your soul is forever gone,
devoured by the greedy crown.

Those truly worthy of the crown
would see it forever locked away,
chained, shackled, gagged, and tortured.
The weakest would be encouraged
to throw stones and make dents.

But Crowns will always rattle the cell doors,
constantly checking the guard's discipline.
We must ensure, if they're ever freed again,
that tarnish and rust are plainly visible
to inspire the next worthy rebels.

Poetry / Zach Czaia

Mark Twain, from Purgatory, 2015

To hell with T. S. Eliot and his love of Huck.
Toni Morrison is right about my book.
They should have kept going down the river.
I regret the way it ended.

In Purgatory do you think all of us dead white writers
are smoking and drinking ourselves into a sweet nostalgia?
We are not.

There is nothing for us but the patience of a new day,
the stroke of it off God's palette.

One day our eyes will open and we will be younger,
in the dawn again, having forgot what made us
avoid the gaze of the one looking at us—
my Jim! my God, what made me flee . . .

We wish we had time, which you have.
We have the wait for
but we do not have time.

Fiction/Sue Bruns

The Mayflower Man

Morning sun slanted through the plate glass window spilling a trapezoid of light across the floor in front of the door. Heat registers against the far wall belched and cracked. The din had died down after the breakfast rush; all but three of the regulars had left for their offices and shops.

Shannon circled past the coffee station, refilled the brewer, grabbed a damp rag from behind the counter. She wiped coffee stains and toast crumbs from the countertop, shook the rag over the metal wastebasket, tossed it into the pan of sudsy water.

These quiet times between meals meant cleaning, refilling and restocking: napkins, condiments, clean cups for behind the counter. Time to drag a damp mop over the peeling linoleum.

The three men in work clothes sat at the table near the front door, sipping their third refills of coffee. Al had said not to offer a fourth refill, even to regulars. The price of coffee was too high for ten-cent bottomless cups. The trio bantered about yesterday's football game, the chances of the Vikings making it to the Superbowl—not about the price of coffee.

"Hey, Nurse!" one yelled, raising his cup toward Shannon and swirling it in a motion she understood. *Too bad, Al,* she thought. *I'm not arguing with these guys about the price of coffee.* She grabbed a pot, circled past them, filled all three cups again.

When no *thank you* came, she pivoted and resumed her route. She'd only worked at the café for a week but already knew several of the regulars—the Greyhound bus driver who seemed interested in the morning cook, the railroad engineer with the diamond willow cane. She hadn't seen these three before.

The bell on the front door's elbow hinge announced the

arrival of a new customer. Shannon slid behind the counter and glanced back to see how many menus to grab: just one. Tucking the menu under her left arm, she tapped a clean glass against the ice dispenser and filled it with water.

The man wore work pants and a crisp, clean shirt with the emblem of Mayflower Trucking Company on its left chest pocket. He walked past the three men at the front table without acknowledgment—*must not be from around here,* she thought. His passing did not, however, go unnoticed. The three men stopped their conversation in mid-stream and paused, freeze-framed, all six eyes following the man as he selected a table not far from theirs and sat, his back to them.

Shannon placed the ice water and menu on the table. "Hi. Coffee?" He nodded. She circled past the first table to get the coffee.

"Hmmmph," she heard as she passed, and then some mumbling, tsks, chatter, snickers and a derisive laugh. Probably some inappropriate comments about her, she thought. She returned with a full cup, passing close by their table. She wouldn't be intimidated.

She set the cup on the table near the Mayflower man's right hand, pulled the pad and pen from her pocket. "Ready to order?" she asked.

The man's voice was low, like thunder, she thought, but clear: "Two eggs over easy, ma'am, please," he said. "Hash browns, wheat toast, bacon, sausage—gravy on the hash browns, and . . . " He reopened the menu and searched the listings. "You got grits, ma'am?"

"What?" she asked.

"Grits."

"I don't believe I know what that is," she said, "so I guess not."

"Never mind," he said, folding the menu shut with his large black hands.

"Sorry," she said.

"Not a problem, ma'am." In the time she had stood there, he had barely looked up. Now he handed her the menu with a quick glance, his dark eyes catching hers only briefly. She tucked the menu under her left arm.

"That'll be up shortly," she said. "Oh, I forgot to ask if you need cream. For your coffee."

"No'm," he said. "I take it black, thanks."

She nodded.

"Takes it black, he said," she heard from the other table, followed by three chuckles.

"Yeah, takes it BLACK," the voice repeated.

The Mayflower man stared into his coffee cup. Shannon shot a look at the table by the door as she took the order to the kitchen. Betty, the morning cook, grabbed the slip, clipped it to a circular rack at eye level, and slid four slices of bacon onto the griddle.

Earlier Shannon had rounded up the half-empty sugar containers and napkin dispensers from the tables and booths to restock. She grabbed the sugar canister from a shelf behind the dining counter to refill the glass dispensers while the Mayflower man's breakfast was cooking.

The three men at the front table didn't seem to be in any hurry to leave. Didn't they have jobs? She glanced toward the table, and the one on the far side closest to the door was staring at her, raising his cup again with that same "come here and fill me up" look. He was the one who had made the unintelligible comment earlier. He had also been the one to make the statement about the Mayflower man liking his coffee black. He'd already had four cups of coffee for a stinking dime. She pretended she hadn't noticed him, intent on the sugar dispensers.

"Hey, Sugar!" she heard. "Coffee here, Girl!" Once again he waved his cup around in the air. She stood, brushing sugar granules from her hands to her apron, slipped behind the counter, plucked the coffee pot from its perch and marched toward the table. The sandy-haired man with the two-day stubble glared at her with impatience, his cup still raised. He set the cup down but slid it across the table as she started to pour, causing her to splash a few drops of coffee on the table.

He laughed with feigned indignation, "Hey, hey!" he said. "Watch out with that hot coffee." The other two men smirked. Shannon stood with the coffee pot poised, waiting for him to take his hand away from the cup before she attempted to pour again. When he didn't, she looked at the other two men to see if they, too, wanted refills. Both slid their hands back and forth, palms down, over their coffee cups in the "no more for me" gesture.

"Hey," the sandy-haired man said, "I'm the one who needs the refill."

"I was just waiting for you to move your hand," she said. "The coffee's hot. I surely don't want to burn you." Her voice was even and steady, the sarcasm as subtle as she could muster, but it wasn't lost on the other two men at the table who "ooohed" at their thirsty friend. He smiled, put both hands up in mock surrender, and Shannon poured half a cup before she moved away.

"Last refill on that old dime," she said. He shot her a look of mock fear and snorted a half laugh.

Betty rang the bell, signaling the order was up, and Shannon set down the pot and went to the kitchen. She ignored the men at the table guffawing about the interaction, grabbed the hot plate from the serving shelf, hustled it across the dining area, and set it down quietly before the Mayflower man.

"Anything else I can get for you?" she asked. "Catsup? More coffee?"

"A little more coffee when you get the chance, please, ma'am," he said.

"BLACK coffee," said the sandy-haired man behind her. "Be sure to make it BLACK."

Shannon returned with the coffee. As she tipped the pot to refill the Mayflower man's cup, the voice behind her said it one more time: "BLACK coffee" and a chortle, a snort from the sandy-haired man.

"BLACK," he said again in a lowered voice, but still loud enough for everyone to hear. "You know," he said to his friends in feigned confidence, "BLACK, to me, is just a really dark Indian."

If the word "black" could have held any more distaste as he spoke it, Shannon thought, it was only beaten by the dripping disgust of the man's inflection on the word "Indian."

She held the coffee pot at the elbow of the Mayflower man, who spoke a soft, steady, "Thank you, ma'am," before beginning his breakfast. Shannon stood, awkwardly paralyzed, unable to walk, to speak, to think. Then she turned toward the table of three and stood just behind the sandy-haired man, coffee pot held high.

"You need any more hot coffee?" she asked. The sandy-haired man was about to answer when one of his friends stood up. "Nope, it's time for us to head back to work, make another dime or two so we can come back."

The three of them kicked back their chairs, grabbed their caps, tossed change on the table and went out the front door.

Poetry/Michael Kiesow Moore

At Home in the Broken Vessel

I have questions about the soul:
Does each soul choose its vessel, from the start?
If a soul had a choice, could it leave
its vessel for another?

I picture a gathering of a few souls,
perhaps over a cup of tea, and
they talk about their own vessels.

One says: *My vessel fails at almost*
everything he does. I don't think I have
seen anyone with a life of such failure,
in every area of his life. I'm not sure
he will ever have a lasting relationship.
The Soul spoke with brimming pride.

Another Soul spoke, also with intense pride:
My vessel made a great mistake.
Driving drunk one night
he accidentally killed a young woman
in a car crash. My vessel is in jail now.

The last Soul jumped in, with as much
boastful pride as the others:
My vessel is in a loveless marriage.
She is stuck in her life in every way
you can imagine. She is sad all the time
and I doubt she will ever choose
what is best for her.

The Souls nod at each other, knowing.

Then with great joy, each returns to
its own broken vessel,
going back to their perfect homes.

Poetry/Peter Stein

Over the Cliff and Through the Fog
(but not necessarily in that order)

The musicality of this moment
must resonate with someone on this planet
but right now a very different wave travels
through my body to find out
what's wrong.

"Wrong" isn't the right word.
"Going on" is the doctor's word choice.
They're not sure either and using unknown rays
to come up with another set of questions:
"Have you noticed a burning sensation in your earlobes at
        night?"
"Does your left testicle become agitated when you walk or
        run?"
"How is your spleen feeling today?"

I'd rather drive off a cliff
than speed through a dense fog.
I could watch the geological life
of the earth flash before my eyes.
Every moment is beautiful from
the right angle, but there's no point
in visiting Big Sur on a foggy day.

A week later the doctor calls me back
to the office and points to a word

> > >

in an incomprehensible dictionary
like it's a Bible verse that will save me
from damnation.
"Treatable" is the only word
I recognize.

Cue the strings.
Choral voices lift
along with the fog.
I see the cliff—
what a view.

Poetry/Nicole Borg

I Have Heard

there is a Chinese proverb
*If you save a man, you are forever
responsible for his life.*
I have also heard there is no such proverb,
a romantic lie authored by Hollywood,
the plot line for a B-movie that sometimes
shows on cable after midnight.

Creative Nonfiction/Ryan M. Neely

No Room for Christmas

Living in the megalopolis known as "The Bay Area" was often filled with moments of roll-your-eyes laughter, the kinds of moments where you can only shake your head and laugh and ask yourself: "Did I really just witness that?" A cynic, as I've often been described, would tell you anytime so many people were crammed together into such tight quarters, the ugly side of humanity is bound to prevail. There's a kind of anonymity living in such a populated area because your neighbors are too busy with their own lives to worry about yours, so it becomes easy to get away with things that the people who live in small towns would be embarrassed to even contemplate. The realist in me, however, would tell you living in a big city will show you humanity in its purest form—not good, not evil, but honest.

Take the blind woman crossing the street against the light. She bounces her cane against the pavement, stopping traffic in all directions (because, really, who wants to be the guy to run over a blind woman—even in such an anonymous city). She hobbles through the crosswalk, like she's been punched in the stomach and can't straighten out. When she's halfway through, someone three cars back lays on their horn. The blind woman stops, turns her head toward the sound, does a double-take, smiles and shouts, "Hey!" and waves at the car. "I'll see you at home," she shouts before flipping her cane over her shoulder and racing across the street.

There are other, simpler stories, like the homeless man lying on the grass in front of the 76 Station on Harrison Street who rolled over onto his side, unzipped, and urinated during rush hour, or the pan handler in North Beach looming from the shadows with a sign that read, PLEASE DONATE TO THE UNITED NEGRO BEER FUND. Stories like these offer fond, if somewhat irksome, memories of life in the city by the bay—memories I would prefer compared to the one which surfaces each time someone asks about my life in San Francisco.

During the summer and winter of 2005 and the spring of 2006, I worked as a mystery shopper for Union 76. It was my job to visit all two hundred 76 Stations in a sixty-mile radius of downtown San Francisco. I was to enter, check the restrooms for cleanliness, buy something worth a dollar, gauge the clerk's level of friendliness, and photograph any transgressions—all without being spotted as a mystery shopper. There was a particular 76 Station on Van Ness Avenue. It was a gas station and service station and sold just enough bagged chips and bottled soda to be considered a convenience store. What the station lacked in variety of products, however, it more than made up in variety of lottery scratch tickets.

It wasn't a surprise to me when I entered the station for the first time and found a couple huddled around the front counter, furiously scratching lottery tickets. After all, nearly every convenience store in the country sells lottery; why should this one be different? What did surprise me, however, was the six-year-old girl, muddy and covered in grease and soot, who held a cup and a cardboard sign with handwritten letters reading, HUNGRY. PLEASE HELP.

My route took me to each station once a month, though the days of the month always varied. Some months I would hit this particular 76 on the third Tuesday, some months it would be the first Wednesday, or the second Thursday. Some days I would arrive at eight in the morning, others not until two in the afternoon. My arrival varied, but what didn't vary was this little girl with her sign sitting next to the front door, or the man and woman huddled around the front counter scratching their lottery tickets.

December was my sixth month as a mystery shopper. I arrived at the Van Ness 76 at nine in the morning on the twenty-third. The girl was there with her sign, the couple inside with their tickets. I made my run, bought a can of soda, and headed back to the car to fill out my report. Something nagged at me about this little girl. It's easy to become calloused and blind to the homeless population when so many panhandlers in the city were charlatans, but shouldn't this girl be in school or day care?

I waited, and watched. Ten minutes later the woman exited the station with a packaged ham sandwich. She handed the sandwich to the girl, then scooped the change out of her cup. The girl tore into her sandwich as if she hadn't eaten in a week. The woman frowned at her and said, "You need to work harder, Mina. Santa cannot bring you presents if Mommy and Daddy can't buy tickets." This was not a roll-your-eyes moment. This was a seethe-with-anger, smash-a-face-with-a-fist moment.

Good thing pragmatism runs through my veins. What good could I do with assault charges? It took the rest of the day to finish my route. For those six hours I mulled over options, and the next day I made a phone call to Child Protective Services. Interfering in the lives of others isn't something I like to do, especially without all the necessary information. For all I knew, the family was perfectly healthy and wealthy, but this time I couldn't help myself.

The woman on the phone thanked me for my tip and promised she'd look into the matter.

When I arrived at the Van Ness Station in January, the girl and her parents weren't there. I never saw them again. I often look back and wonder if I did the right thing. In a city this large, anonymity is a shield protecting everyone from shame and ridicule, and ignorance is a weapon used to punish those who do things differently. I was ignorant and anonymous; I struck out without all the information and was protected from any backlash but my own conscience.

Poetry/David Eric Northington

The Starving Child

Numb from lack of attention
The starving child waits alone
Cold back bedroom isolated
Headphones block the silent parents
Robert Plant gives "No Quarter"
Elton John sings "Funeral for a Friend"
Vinyl spins 'round and 'round
Like his fourteen-year-old life
He switches albums seeking answers
In his dead brother's records
Listening for meaning or explanation
And finds nothing

Poetry/Sue Reed Crouse

The Amazing Invisible Girl and Her Father Play a Game

She sees herself as the tiny push
of air that rain displaces. Unless
you look for the cartwheel

of white-backed leaves,
you won't see her.

She blows into the house
through the aluminum "A"
on the screen door and tries

to turn into a girl. With all her might;
she manages a shadow which blends

into black and white TV images
and newsprint. Her father relaxes
on the couch behind the *Free Press*,

and doesn't hear her voice
because his deaf ear can't catch soft sounds.

The amazing invisible girl, desperate
to play, places her old stuffed rabbit
on her dad's tired foot and waits

and waits. Without lowering the paper,
he flips Bun into the air, where it hits the wall

and falls to the floor. She retrieves
her toy, delighted, and wraps the rabbit's
human-like arms around her neck.

Poetry/Jeanne Emrich

Laugh Lines

They are not laugh lines, you say,
but the lines artists get when they squint,
the better to see their subjects.
Get rid of the details and the truth of the thing
will stare right back at you, ready for the brush.

So why, when we are together, do you
throw your head back, your throat erupting
with little whoops and barks and, yes, snorts
of surprised delight? Why do you always
complain that the muscles in your cheeks
burn from the strain of unrelieved merriment?

No, it's laughter that put those lines
around your eyes. Laughter, that extreme sport
for the face; laughter, when tears won't do;
laughter that shrugs off pain; laughter, which is
the heart helplessly succumbing to wit.
And your lines, well—they are very deep
are they not?

Fiction/Michael McCormick

Cass at Eighty-Three

Serene, oblivious, Cass aimed her car at the semi's bumper. The Volvo clung to the big rig like a remora on a shark.

The speedometer read eighty-three mph.

James knew Cass had replaced so many parts of her car that, like Theseus's ancient ship, none of the original remained. He suddenly wondered if the airbags worked.

"Extreme drafting," Cass explained, misreading the look of adrenal concentration on James's face. "I'm so deep into this guy's slipstream the friction is near zero. It's almost a vacuum."

"Then how can we breathe?" James asked, although suffocation seemed the least likely cause of death at that moment.

Cass shrugged. She rested one hand on the wheel while the other plundered her purse for a cigarette. Lung cancer being another unlikely cause of death at the moment.

James forced his gaze away from the Grim Reaper and his Peterbilt mud flaps. On a hill he saw three cell towers arranged like the crosses on Golgotha, signifying competing empires of AT&T, Sprint, and Verizon.

"Skull Hill," said Cass, sporadic telepathy being one of her talents. "That's what Golgotha means. It sounds like a Nancy Drew book. Or a death metal band?"

James watched Golgotha recede into the realm of Objects Nearer Than They Appear. But inevitably his attention returned to the trailer doors that filled their field of vision. At last the dam broke, and he blurted out the uncool question:

"What if the truck makes a sudden stop?"

Another shrug.

"He knows I'm here," Cass said. "We made eye contact in his mirror."

Unable to stop himself now, James flung his last shreds of dignity into the roaring wind:

"What if he's one of those psycho killer truckers?"

Cass appeared to consider this possibility.

"You're right," she announced.

She threw the Volvo into fourth gear, its engine keening in disbelief. The truck shot away from them like a marlin snapping a fishing line.

"Grab the wheel," said Cass.

She released the steering wheel but kept her foot on the gas. She peered into her purse. James grabbed the wheel. He tried to keep the Volvo in its lane while traffic surged around them. Horns bleated.

"Found them!" Cass declared, waving a crumpled green pack of Newports.

She struck a match, lit a cigarette, and resumed driving all in one flowing movement. Menthol smoke filled the car.

"Those things will kill you," said James, releasing his grip on the steering wheel.

Cass considered it.

"Unlikely," was her verdict, as she shifted back to fifth.

Poetry/Justin Watkins

Netting Suckers

We rose before dawn in cold dark spring
Drove forgotten two-track roads
Through forest canopy to dim corridors of water
To stand as brothers in pushing current
Landing nets held fast between our legs

Upstream Cousin poled fish forward
From the calm of their deep holds
From the silted pool bellies
They fled downstream riding hope
But there was only our waiting gauntlet

Suckers: the dark elongates
Dark like my memory of the stream
Cold darkness fluid and smooth
Came to our nets not apart from water
But as shadows born of it

From stream bank to rough burlap sacks
From the forest to the back lawn
We used heavy dull knives
To make rough cuts along spines
The blood is in the grass that still grows

Splayed brined fish meat
Arranged in a block smokehouse
And a fire set to smolder
Our corporeal beings flesh and bone
Can be traced back

> > >

To swimming white suckers
That followed an old instruction
To run upstream with the lengthening day
Against the pushing current
Through wooded dark

Poetry/Mark Traynor

Dusk at the Fair

Strollers full of toddlers
leave with the midday heat,
their clammy limbs dangle,
faces smeared, reddening.
The salty sweet breezes
mix with barn hay, pork smoke,
midway silhouettes turn,
fall and rise as I scan
the purpling sky and burst
like a new autumn star.

Poetry/James Bettendorf

Well Lived Bookstore

Browsing a shelf of used books, mysteries
and love stories, I find you. Aromas
of memories, musty, dusty pages,
a classic, that had been loved. A real page-

turner, I can't put you down. Pages dog-
eared, still a great epic, the prose unmatched,
the language, clear-spoken, is beautiful.
So difficult at times to understand,

I love the challenge, and the heroine
holds my interest. I, the lucky reader,
peruse it again, the story so rich,
the climax never fails to surprise. I
never want it to end so I read more
slowly each time and savor the story.

Poetry/ **Reprinted from Talking Stick 7, 1998/*
Carson T. Gardner

Hummingbird Feather

*

Hummingbird feather,
so light in my clumsy hand,
far shorter than my lifeline,
softer than a breath;
its owner passed over,
her little fire so soon gone out.
This fragile miracle—
small, perfect, iridescent quill
borrowed from its fellows—
in its place imparting joyful freedom
to the smallest mystery
of eagle's nation in the sky.
Hummingbird feather,
like a child's bright fantasy
in my calloused palm;
a gentle reminder
that good things
are possible
with dreams gently anchored
by love,
because there is more
to hope
than feathers in the sky.

Fiction/*Honorable Mention*/P. Helen Kester

The Living Room

"Do you have to use the oven when it's ninety degrees out?" John washed his hands at the kitchen sink. Motor oil and grease swirled down the drain.

Doris turned the oven off and removed the casserole. She could have fried hamburgers for their dinner though there was only enough ground beef for one small one for each of them. She had no buns and Wonder Bread made a poor substitute. John would have left the table hungry and angry.

Mixing the beef with macaroni, peas, and chopped celery meant there would be enough to fill their stomachs. The price was a hot kitchen.

"How was your day?" she asked. She knew how his day was. How every day was. He hated his job at the automotive shop. Perhaps if she showed that she cared and empathized it might put him in a better mood. He might not react so badly when she told him.

"How do you think it was?" He threw the black-stained towel at the rack and missed. It fell in a damp heap on the floor.

Paula entered the room carrying her transistor radio, bopping to the beat of "Rock Around the Clock."

"Shut that crap off," said her stepfather. Paula hit the off button quickly.

Doris despaired of improving his mood. Yet this couldn't wait another day.

Doris called the boys to the table.

Jeff helped Bobby perch on the telephone books that lifted him high enough to reach the tabletop.

"You've got to eat more than that." John scooped a spoonful of hotdish onto his stepson's plate next to the mound of strawberry Jell-O lying there.

Jeff didn't look up from his plate. "I'm maintaining my weight," he mumbled. "I've got a match tomorrow."

"You still gotta eat something."

Jeff shrugged.

Paula moved her food around with a fork. Bobby seemed pleased with the white ball he had made from a slice of Wonder Bread.

"You'll sit there until that plate is clean." John pointed at Bobby. "I work damn hard to put food on this table."

Doris conceded that John did work hard but the corner bar saw more of his earnings than his family did. She didn't earn much as a waitress but at least her earnings were steady and she brought them home.

John leaned back in his chair when he'd finished eating and belched mightily. He rose and walked toward the living room.

"Bring me a cup of coffee, will ya?"

Doris watched his retreating back and glanced at the coffeepot on the stove that he had just passed.

Suppose I dropped dead. Could he pour his own coffee then?

Paula rose and reached for her stepfather's cup.

"I'll get it." Doris picked up the cup and filled it with hot coffee. She added milk and sugar and followed her husband.

The room John retired to, adjacent to the kitchen, was dominated by an old television set, balanced on a rickety metal tubing stand. The rest of the furniture, sagging and worn, formed an audience for the TV. No one but John sat in the only easy chair in the room, even when he wasn't home.

For another family at another time this room served as a dining room. The built-in buffet, chair rail, and dark green wallpaper declared its authentic role. But for this family of five, forced to manage in a two-bedroom apartment, a dining room would have been a frivolous accommodation. Instead, the dining room became the living room, and the actual living room became the required third bedroom.

John had turned on the TV, removed his shoes, and unbuttoned his pants. He sat with his feet propped up on the coffee table.

Doris gave the coffee to her husband and returned to the kitchen. The kids put their dishes in the sink and departed to their rooms.

Doris took her time cleaning up. When there were no more chores to perform, she filled a mug with black coffee and joined her husband in front of the television. She tucked her skinny frame into the corner of the sofa nearest John's easy chair and held her mug with both hands.

John's cigarette burned in an ashtray on the coffee table. Doris lit her own, and glanced furtively at her husband between puffs. During a commercial, she spoke with feigned casualness.

"There's not enough money for the rent."

The scar on John's jaw, carved by a broken bottle wielded by his father when John was only twelve years old, bulged as he clenched his teeth. News programming returned with a report that President Eisenhower had sent military advisers to a never-before-heard-of country somewhere halfway around the world.

John turned to look at Doris. "What the hell do you do with the money I give you?" His voice was so low Doris could barely understand the tight sounds. She offered her rehearsed response.

"I got groceries this week, paid the electric bill, and there was Bobby's medicine . . . "

"I work my ass off for you and those kids." John shoved his feet into his shoes and began tying the laces. Doris pressed herself into the fabric of the sofa.

John rose quickly from his chair. Doris flinched. "That's right. You better be afraid."

He buttoned his pants and headed out of the room. Doris heard him cross the kitchen and slam the back door. A moment later a car engine sounded and droned away.

Doris sat trembling. How long before he would return and how bad would the beating be this time?

She sat for a few minutes allowing her heartbeat and breathing to return to near normal, her body to stop shaking. *You have to get out!*

Doris set her mug on the coffee table next to John's, beside the ashtray that still held his abandoned cigarette. She snuffed it out and moved quickly down the hall, past the bedrooms and bathroom, to the living room that wasn't a living room. She reached into the wardrobe where she couldn't see it, but knew an old suitcase lay in the clutter on the floor. She felt its rough, pebbly surface and remembered when she had used it two years earlier. The memory hit her so hard she needed to sit down. With her elbows on her knees, she pressed the heels of her hands against her eyes. Blue and yellow blotches danced.

It had been a cold winter night. They boarded the first bus leaving the depot to a town she didn't know and had never seen. All four of them pressed into one seat. Bobby cried until he had the hiccups and couldn't stop hiccupping. Doris had used rent money to buy the tickets. That earned her another beating.

The bus pulled up to a breakfast stop the following morning. Before they got off the bus, Doris saw John's beat-up Pontiac roll into the parking lot. Bobby stood on the seat to press against the bus window. "Daddy! Daddy," he called.

John got out from behind the wheel and stood beside the car, feet planted wide, arms folded. Doris hesitated behind the protection of the window glass. Bobby broke free of her hold, toddled through the open door, and ran to his father. John hoisted his son up. Bobby buried his face in John's neck and happily kicked his feet. John kept his gaze on his wife's face behind the glass that separated them.

Doris turned to her two older children. None of them said a word as they disembarked the bus and took their seats in the rusty Pontiac. John plopped Bobby on Doris's lap as he crawled in behind the wheel. He started the engine and aimed the car toward home. Later John threatened to kill her if she ever tried to take his only son away from him again.

With a shuddering sigh, Doris rose and returned the suitcase to the dark corner of the closet. Another sigh brought the tears under control. She went to the bathroom, pressed some cold water on her eyes, and patted her face dry with a frayed towel.

She peeked into the boys' bedroom. Jeff was propped up in his bed reading comics. Bobby played with toy trucks on the floor making *burrr burrr* sounds through wet lips. Paula's door was closed. She was doing homework or reading the *True Confession* magazines she hid under her bed.

Back in the living room, Doris sat on the sofa and reached for the telephone. She dialed a number. After the third ring, she heard her brother's voice on the line.

"Matt," she began. "I don't have enough money for the rent again. I hate to ask . . . "

Poetry/Susan Perala-Dewey

Remembering Cornucopia

Oh how I miss the indigo blue of summer setting its mood
On Lake Superior and you, walking hand in hand
Along the sand, rocks, and rib cages of driftwood
Our bodies glow against the crest of scarlet peach
Wanting only to cling to the thorax woven between us
In the black of night, soft and warm as cashmere

In the black of night, soft and warm as cashmere
Oh how I miss the indigo blue of summer setting its mood
Wanting only to cling to the thorax woven between us
On Lake Superior and you, walking hand in hand
Our bodies glow against the crest of scarlet peach
Along the sand, rocks, and rib cages of driftwood

Along the sand, rocks, and rib cages of driftwood
In the black of night, soft and warm as cashmere
Our bodies glow against the crest of scarlet peach
Oh how I miss the indigo blue of summer setting its mood
On Lake Superior and you, walking hand in hand
Wanting only to cling to the thorax woven between us

Oh how I miss you and I walking hand in hand on Lake
        Superior
We glow scarlet peach against indigo blue.

Poetry/Marlys Guimaraes

The Thermometer Reads 22 Degrees Below Zero

There's a chill in the house.
I put on my goose down parka,
the old one, with matted fur on the hood
that smells like wood smoke,
don the black face mask I wore yesterday,
and put on dirty work gloves.

I am going outside to feed the fire.
No need to dress fancy, soon I will have orbs
of smoke around my head as I open the
heavy door and throw chunks and logs
of pine and birch into its belly.

I choose to stay outside, listen to boot tracks
creak with each step of frozen snow,
visit the hen house to spread extra treats
to keep them warm, sunflower seeds, cracked
corn, and chunks of crusty old bread.

It's cold for the redpolls, blue jays, chickadees
and peckers of wood as they gather around
the feeder. They fly away when I approach
with my pail, but soon return like Sunday
congregations waiting for sacraments.

The birds are fed, the eggs gathered,
a fire blazes in the outdoor furnace.
I've augured the ashes from the cone and
still, I want to stay outside.

> > >

I walk the fence line identifying tracks
of rabbit and squirrel, then wonder about the
small paw prints and the cries of coyote
I heard in the night.

I should go inside. I am away from my
phone. Someone may need cheering or
a listening ear or words of comfort.
Still I walk, watching the sun as moon.

Some days I am 22 degrees below zero.

Fiction/Kathleen Lindstrom

Fired Up

I'm good at fitting in.

I sit over there, by the window that overlooks the parking lot. See the philodendron on top of the file cabinet? That's my cube. Three rows down, turn left and there you are. Eight feet by six, a desk, a chair, one four-drawer file cabinet, two overhanging bookcases, a hook for my coat, a PC and one visitor's chair. That's where I work.

One day I felt daring. So I pulled in an extra chair from an empty cube just to be different for a change. But Pamela, the Facilities manager, found it while patrolling the building one night and told my boss it had to go. *Only Class 10 employees can have two chairs in a cube*, she said. I'm still a Class 8.

In fact, I've been Class 8 for almost fourteen years now. My title is systems payroll coordinator; and I'm the one who enters your weekly time sheet data, so you get paid on time. There are six of us, one for each division. We're a huge company. It's an important job.

But every job is important. That's what they always tell us. "No job is too small," my boss will say at the end of each department meeting. "Everyone makes a difference. Now let's get back to work."

Betty Jacobs sits in the cube next to mine. Ralph Noren sits across the aisle. Betty is on the phone all day, keeping track of her teenaged son. Ralph just got promoted and will be moving to a bigger cube at the end of the month. He'll be a senior systems payroll coordinator, which is a Class 9 and entitles him to more money and an extra two-drawer file cabinet.

I applied for that job, but didn't get it. Ralph has a degree and I don't—at least that's how my boss explained it when I complained. It's the sixth promotion I've tried for and didn't get. I'm very discouraged.

I'm a good employee, don't get me wrong. My error rate is

only two percent, the best in our department. I'm in my cube before eight every morning. I never leave before five. I haven't taken a sick day in three-and-a-half years. My reports are compiled and sent to corporate personnel every Wednesday by noon. I'm dedicated to my job and do everything I'm told.

In fact, at my last evaluation, when my boss said I looked too glum and unapproachable, I plastered a permanent smile on my face to show how happy I was to be there and what a good team player I am.

But it still didn't get me promoted.

My mother is not surprised. "You're a forty-six-year-old woman," she keeps reminding me. "And it's a hard, hard world out there. It gets harder when you lose your looks. I told you to marry Marvin when you had the chance."

My mother and I still live in our lifelong home on Edgeview Road. It's a two-bedroom bungalow big enough for the two of us and our cat, Lucy. But what my mother doesn't know is that Marvin dumped me for a thirty-two-year-old woman with two kids he met at some bar—and then married six months later.

This happened in May. I'm still trying to get my head around the whole thing. We'd been dating for almost eleven years; so, as you might guess, being unattached again is a big change in my life. It was always understood we'd eventually get married. Well, it was my understanding, anyway. Marvin is a long-haul truck driver who's on the road five days a week. We'd get together every Saturday, go to a movie, a restaurant, watch TV and then make love.

I liked the predictability of our routine and was a good girlfriend to Marvin. He was a quiet person, just like me. He didn't ask for much, just a little tenderness once in a while, which, I'm told, is something all men really need.

So what more did he want?

As you can probably see, I'm beginning to ask that question a lot lately. *Just what do they **want**?*

Maybe everyone in our company is asking the same thing

right now. Some strange things have been happening lately that have management on edge. I can almost see them scratching their heads, wondering "What's going on here? What should we do? What are we doing wrong?"

I know the feeling.

Yesterday, for example, the fire alarm went off and a booming voice ordered everyone to leave the building. "This is an emergency," it said. "This is not a practice drill."

So we all grabbed our coats and, with hundreds of us packed in the stairwell, moved like sludge from the tenth down to the first floor and eventually out into the parking lot. A fire truck arrived, followed by the bomb squad unit and a German shepherd tugging on the leash of its no-nonsense handler. After shivering in the cold for an hour or so, after trying to carry on a casual conversation with my coworkers, after finally finding myself alone, standing outside their chatty little circle, Security ordered us back into the building.

A hoax, they told us later. Someone with a grudge trying to sabotage the company. It even made last night's news.

Imagine that. We were on Channel 6.

So, this morning, Betty pops up from her chair to greet me as I walk in.

Actually, it's not so much a greeting as her way of letting me know she got here first. It's become a game between us. Who gets to work the earliest? Who gets our boss's attention as the eager beaver, the early bird, the good girl in his happy little group?

It used to be me. Now, if I'm not here by 7:15, it's Betty who shines.

"Did you see Channel 6 last night?" she asks, pretending to ignore the sticky ooze of competition gluing us together.

"Sure did," I say with my permanent smile. "I wonder how they got those shots. I never saw any cameras around."

"It's kinda scary," she adds. "First those two fires in the bathrooms. Now a bomb scare. Who do you think it could be?"

She's right. It *is* getting scary. We'd been evacuated two

other times in the past month because someone set fires in the women's bathrooms on the third floor, then on the tenth. It's easy enough to do. You just light up a paper towel when no one's around, drop it in the wastebasket, let it simmer for a while, let the fire catch hold, and then, *whoof,* watch it all go up in flames.

"Don't know," I say. "But someone sure doesn't like it here."

"Well, what *really* bugs me," she says, "is the person who is still stealing lunches out of the refrigerator. I'd like to find out who it is and then wring their sneaky little neck."

"Still?" I ask, knowing she knows it's not a problem for me. I eat in the cafeteria and never bring food from home.

"Yesterday, I brought a pecan pie for dessert and someone snatched it right out of my bag. They left the damn apple and carrot sticks, but took away my home-made pie!"

I shake my head, pretending to share her fury at the unfairness of it all.

"I don't care if they blow up the building," she laughs. "Just keep their dirty little hands off my home-made pie."

We chuckle at that, knowing she's kidding, realizing the requisite chit-chat between us is done for the day. Then we get down to work.

As my computer warms up, I unlock my desk. The pie is still there, probably not as fresh, but that's okay. I'll nibble on it now and then when Ralph and Betty aren't around.

Oh, and there are the matches—tucked under last week's printouts, piled high, down deep in the back of my bottom drawer.

But you're probably not surprised at that. As I said, I'm good at fitting in. And with my new-found permanent smile, I'm thinking anything is possible.

Poetry/Kathleen Pettit

Query

The cold north wind blows away mists
     of lovers and other sorrows
     of friends and works well done
     of histories known and hidden follies
leaving a landscape barren even of detritus.

On what will we build?

From where will the shimmering waves of air on
     a clear sunlit morning come?

How will the breath of the earth rise up to shape
     new stories?

Will we be always destined to repeat old battles
     that leave us to wonder why
     once again, we have lost?

Poetry/Adrian S. Potter

Only the Moon Knows You're Singing the Blues

The ghosts of your misguided passions
haunt you like unanswered questions.
How many years have you wandered?
And what are you searching for—not love
or faith seemingly denoting some destination
to sprint towards, but a song piping its way
soulfully through the pink conduit of your throat
like first breath, a blessed exaltation in knowing
exactly how to convert your angst into amens.

Whisper your name to document your existence,
exercise your lungs in praise of everything you desire
but cannot obtain. Doubt inhabits the space
surrounding you, steels the tender night air
as hope gradually vanishes like cigar smoke.

Happiness is a fossil buried deep beneath you,
weathered and beat to the earth with old sorrows,
hollow promises. You are the accidental catalyst
that flips the world over and over like a tarnished coin,
draped in the fabric of temptation hemmed together
by the devil's finest needlework. Venture where you must.
The sun will rise there. The water will flow.
Take inventory of places, names, faces.
Living is how you practice dying.
Keep a flickering light near your heart,
as the dull thunder of desperation
traces each step, maps every movement.
Only the moon knows you're singing the blues,
while the world thinks you're smiling at its shine.

Poetry/Sharon Harris

All-Class Reunion

the hottest night of the summer—
the Legion is swarming with old classmates
from decades of school years.

drinks and more drinks—
laughter flows with the liquor;
I stay sticky with sweat
from hugs and embraces.

I walk through the crowds,
seeing faces familiar
and some too changed to recognize.
many classmates are gone now
and some haven't shown up
since graduation.
some locals avoid this completely
while others travel miles to be here.

I like wondering
about the crazy parties
I never attended.
I like wondering
who met and stayed together for the long haul,
who had one-night stands,
who has slept with whom,
who had a baby by one boyfriend
but married another and the men never knew.

I wonder which couples broke up years ago
but still feel that special jolt

> > >

when back in each other's sight.
I watch them
as memories like magnets pull them together
from clear across the room.

I wonder which ones are glad the way they went,
which ones have regrets the size of life,
which ones still have silent yearnings
like I do.

Poetry/Susu Jeffrey

Love Seat

Someone who will be at the airport
and dinner
who writes steam hearts
on the bathroom mirror.
I want someone to plant trees with.

My idea of beauty
is smile lines.
The idea of communication
is to not
have to say it all
   all the time.

Creative Nonfiction/Katherine Schaefer

Shelter

I wait to turn on the television until Tom leaves for his morning class. He's running late, and his red Camaro fishtails on the gravel as it pulls out of the driveway. The TV is an old black and white I found by the dumpster behind my apartment in Minneapolis. A note taped to the screen said PLEASE TAKE, so I did. It hardly works, pulling in just two channels, three on a clear day, and there's so much fuzz and snow you can barely make out what's on the screen. But the TV voices fill the silence in this little house Tom is renting out in the country while he takes agri-business classes in Waseca.

Tom doesn't know anybody here. I told him if he lived in the dorms he'd meet people, make friends, but he refused to get a dorm room. Instead, he found this place, out west of town. It's more of a shack than a farmhouse, since there's no farm to go along with it—no barn or sheds or cropland, only a falling-down garage. For company, Tom got a dog from the shelter, a young brown mutt dumped by someone who didn't want it once its puppy cuteness wore off. Tom named him Buddy; I don't care for the name, but my opinion doesn't count because it's not my dog. Buddy could grow into a nice dog someday, but he's young and bored, trapped like I am out here in Tom's rental house with nothing to do all day. Buddy barks and whines and chews on everything, so Tom shuts him up in a spare room off the kitchen until the scratching on the door drives me crazy. The room is unheated except for whatever warmth filters in from the rest of the house, so when Tom shuts Buddy in for the night, it just gets colder and colder. Tom threw a carpet remnant—ugly swirls of red and gold and black—down on the floor for the dog to sleep on.

"It's so cold in there," I say when I go check on Buddy, set down bowls of food and water.

"He's a dog," Tom says back. "When you were out on the

THE TALKING STICK VOLUME 25

farm, you never even let your dog in the house at all."

"True," I say. "But he slept in the barn during the winter, in with the cows."

"He's just a dog," Tom says again. "He's fine."

Now I open the door and Buddy springs out and runs in circles around me, jumping up on my legs. Cold air from the room seeps along the floor, bringing with it the reek of dog shit. I fish a piece of cardboard from the trash and scoop up a pile of turds, then fling them out the front door into the snowy yard. Back in Buddy's room, I lift a corner of the carpet remnant, but it's stuck to the floorboards by partly frozen dog pee, the rubber backing saturated with crystalline shards. I go back out to the kitchen, shutting the door behind me.

"Don't worry," I tell Buddy, who pushes his flank hard against my knees. "I won't make you go in there all day."

It's a Monday and I should be back in the Cities at my own classes, but I'm stuck here in Waseca. On Friday, Tom drove up to fetch me for the weekend, and then on Sunday when it was time to take me back, he said he was too tired, didn't feel like driving all that way. Why didn't I stay another day? Just skip my Monday classes?

But I don't want to skip again. Art history is on Monday morning, and then drawing all afternoon, and I love both classes. I've skipped twice already this semester, when Tom did the same thing, bringing me down here for the weekend and then refusing to take me back on time. We've argued about it, more than once.

"I'll buy my own car so I can come and go as I please," I say.

"Go ahead then," he says back. Neither of us mentions that I'm the one who paid for his Camaro out of my inheritance, but the fact hangs heavy.

"Or I'll take the bus," I say. Of course, first I'd have to find out where the bus depot is in Waseca, and figure out the schedule, which isn't so easy since Tom doesn't have a phone.

"And how do you think you're getting to the bus station?"

he says. "Because I'm not taking you."

"I'll walk," I say.

"Yeah, right," he says. "Well, get going already, I'm not stopping you."

But I always stay. What would happen to Buddy if I left? Would Tom lock him in that cold, stinking room forever? Would he neglect to feed and water him? Or would he throw open the front door and fling the dog out into the world, as unwanted as before it came from the shelter?

Now, looking back on that winter Monday, I'd like to give my eighteen-year-old self some backbone. If this were fiction, I'd turn her into a spunky, likable heroine, have her filch the keys out of Tom's pocket and repossess that Camaro she paid for, gather up that sweet brown dog and drive back to the Cities and the art classes she loved. But that's not what happened. What was I doing with a person who got a dog from a shelter and then failed to *give* it shelter? Who named his dog Buddy and then failed to treat it as one?

The truth is, I felt sorrier for the dog than I did for myself, recognizing Buddy's sense of abandonment and entrapment, and his hunger for love. But I could not yet recognize my own sense of abandonment after my parents' deaths, and my need for someone to take me in, no matter the price I would pay before I could see my own self-worth.

Poetry/Jan Chronister

Yardwork

Gardens conceal
bare dirt where children's
shoes dragged slowing down on swings
tell-tale depression over old septic tank,
spot where the cat died.

Every ten years or so
I dig down to clay
greasy and red
tug out balsam roots
rocks missed the first time.

I cart it all away
shovel in fresh dirt
bury daffodils waxy as candles
and wait.

Poetry/*Reprinted from Talking Stick 12, 2003/*
Norma Thorstad Knapp

Skipping Stones

I watch children by the water choose a pocketful of stones,
lay them neatly in one long line,
then fling them one by one with concentrated care.
I watch, remember, and think I know
the science of skipping stones:
how to select the right stone, flat, with one smooth side
so surface repels surface
and stone leaps high like a graceful dancer;
how to hold it in the forefinger's crook
and flip it off the finger's tip,
so stone strides out and turns
through pirouettes of strength and swirl;
how to figure the angle and speed of the arm's fling
and so increase the skips to five or six or even more.
I carefully select a stone of my own, toss it with confidence,
watch it jump, stumble . . . slip out of sight. Astonished,
I wonder what ability
what competence,
not calculable,
can deny
the science of
skipping stones?

Poetry/Eric Chandler

Get Off My Lawn

They rang my doorbell
and ran.
After several weeks of it,
my daughter asked,
"Am I going to be abducted?"
That was that.

I snuck out in the dark
and caught them.
I told them to
stay out of my yard.
I put profanity mustard
on that sandwich.

They told me
their actual names.
They were too stupid to bolt,
too stupid to lie.
Back in my day,
we would've done both.

Fiction/Cindy Fox

Beauty Fix

A messy side-part hid my gray roots, the best hairstyling advent since the ponytail. But my dyed ash blonde hair, dry and crunchy, sucked rust from our well water like a thirsty sponge. With a metallic taste in my mouth, I gritted my teeth and vowed to stop coloring my hair. But to grow out my hair and go natural wasn't an easy decision. My mind was fraught with questions, bouncing back and forth like a ping pong game: "*Should I, or shouldn't I?*" When I slammed the ball down and decided I should, worrywart me couldn't stop thinking what people would say when they passed me on the street: "*Does she, or doesn't she?*"

I threw those questions out the window when a flashy, red pick-up truck hugged my tail as I drove to the market. In the rearview mirror I saw three teenaged boys smirking and elbowing each other. From their vantage point, I looked like a young woman with shoulder-length blonde hair with funky orange highlights. The truck lurched into the left lane and cruised alongside me, jerking back and forth, teasing me to look over. When our eyes met, the driver tromped on the gas. Their startled faces were lost in a cloud of blue diesel exhaust, the roar of dual pipes mimicking their howling laughter.

Eight months after tossing my last box of hair color in the garbage, I fought the urge to visit the landfill to retrieve it. Demoralized, I held a magnifying mirror two inches from my nose and searched for glints of silver *highlights* in my hair. Despite the chocolate brown lowlights my hairdresser had added to soften the blow of growing out my hair, the chocolate kept melting away. My crown looked like I was wearing a mousy brown skull cap with gray hair springing up for air. "*Jeez,*" I pouted to myself. "*I want more hair, not mohair.*"

I squinted through side-swept bangs my stylist had insisted were the rage and would camouflage my male pattern baldness, which had no business invading my turf. My bangs didn't sweep, but instead dusted my nose with static electricity. I jammed in a bobby pin to lift them up and was shocked how the mirror, like a microscope, enlarged the cracks and crevices on my face. My crow's feet looked like the bird landed with a firm grip, clawing deep before letting go. My laugh lines were like craters, my cheeks sagging from a prolonged drought with no collagen.

My drab hair did nothing to enhance my skin tone, but definitely highlighted my age spots, which could not be misconstrued as beauty marks. Disgusted at my reflection, I grabbed the phone and scheduled an appointment for the next day. The hair salon at the mall locked me in for their first opening, noon on Sunday.

Haley, bless her soul, worked at the salon on the day most people have off. She sweetly asked, "What can I do for you today?"

Like an erupting volcano, I slammed my limp bangs, receding hairline, and lowlights that had run down the drain. I paused to catch my breath, handing her a picture clipped from a magazine of a chic woman with puffy bangs and wisps framing her face and neck.

"I want to look like her," I said. "And can you somehow blend the ends that look like they've been soaking in a bowl of chlorine bleach?"

"Sure," she said, running her fingers through my hair. "I can do something similar to a razor cut but I won't use a razor that can damage dry hair like yours."

Haley shampooed my hair, her fingers dancing in perfect time to the soft rock lilting from the sound system. My eyes drifted shut; my tight neck muscles unwound as my head sagged into the sink. I didn't want to move, but Haley coaxed me up and escorted me to her chair.

I winced at my reflection in the wall mirror, the unforgiving fluorescent lights shadowing the fissures on my face. My drooping eyelids poked my eyes deeper under my crease-lined forehead. Puffy bags under my eyes looked like I'd been on an all-night bender. My hair was slicked back, baring two bald spots that looked like pockets on a pool table. I cringed, praying no one would see me like this.

The salon phone rang and Haley rushed off as she was working double-duty as a receptionist too. While waiting, I scrutinized my image in the mirror. The billowing cape accentuated my long neck with its crepe-paper skin I hid behind a turtleneck whenever I went out in public. I thought, *"How incongruous that a turtleneck can hide a chicken neck. Don't turtles have wrinkled necks too?"*

Haley was back and I compared our reflections, the young and the old. Haley's smooth, tight skin was like a baby's, light years away from the ravages of gravity that will tug and pull at her skin. Her short pixie cut bared her face and neck, and I envied her youth.

My hair was one long snarl that hung on tight like a rebellious child's first visit to the doctor. A spray of relaxing serum released the tangles and Haley's comb slid through my thin tresses. She pulled off matted hair after each stroke which reminded me of my clogged-up drain last week.

The plumber ran a snake through the pipes and captured two clumps of greasy hair the size of billiard balls hanging out at a joint leading to the sewer. I chewed on my lower lip and wondered if I *was* going bald.

Haley cut two inches from my length and the reddish-yellow ends floated to the floor like autumn leaves. After slicing strips below the demarcation line of my two-toned mop, she swung the chair around. It was time to cut my bangs.

"Do you think I should do this?" I asked. "It's taken so long to grow them this long."

"Well, I've been cutting your hair to look like that pretty girl in the picture, but it's up to you."

My indecisiveness crumbled when I heard *pretty*, and said, "Go for it."

I watched the first snip and then closed my eyes as my side-swept bangs fluttered down my face in the direction they'd always wanted to go. Bang, bang and they all fell down. Finally our battle was over.

Haley twirled the chair and handed me a mirror. My new cut had lifts and curves in all the right places and I didn't look like I was wearing a bowl on my head anymore. My bangs were back, right where I wanted them to be, hiding my expanding forehead. I padded her tip an extra 5 percent, then wandered the mall for some much-needed retail therapy.

I smiled at my image in the shop windows, and entered a clothing store that catered to gals half my age. I tried on a fashionable print hoodie with rhinestone studs that promised a sparkling impression. The clerk suggested a mauve turtleneck that matched a hue in the jacket. When she marveled how the rosy color brightened my skin tone, how could I walk away from that?

Her compliment steered me into a beauty supply store. I filled my shopping basket with an exfoliating scrub to whisk dead skin off my face and a lift serum that proclaimed miraculous anti-gravity rejuvenation while I slept. And, finally, an anti-wrinkle cream the lady behind the counter assured me would erase ten years from my age.

Heading to the checkout counter, I stopped by the hair color products aisle. I backed away, but couldn't resist the pull of an aisle sign arm waving me over. *Semi-permanent Hair Color.* I grabbed a bottle from the shelf and read the label: *Perfect for gray-blending and subtle color.* I looked down both ends of the aisle and the human eye behind a security camera must have sounded an alert somewhere to nab a shoplifter. A sales girl was suddenly beside me offering assistance. No, I didn't need her help. My eyes swept the aisle one more time. When I was sure there was no one I knew in the store, I perused the color chart. I chose a brown shade with tints of yellow like the hair of a newborn deer, a color so natural no one would ever know.

Back home, my giddiness dissolved like a Coke that had lost its fizz. I'd broken my vow like an addict craving a temporary fix. But I promised myself this would be the last time, knowing old age had slapped my face with wrinkles and I'd continue growing older waiting for them to disappear. Knowing when the dye and yet more hair swirled down the drain, I will resolve to age gracefully. I will love the heavy-lidded woman in the mirror and neatly tuck the yellow remnants of her youth in a bun.

Poetry/Ronald j. Palmer

Poem for a Woman Who Walks Her Dog by My House, Daily, Sometimes We Even Chat

I started to write a poem about you
decided better not to pursue.
I have a wife, you a boyfriend;
I am a late fifty-eight, you thirty or twenty-two.

I had a beginning but not an end,
a sentiment with no way to send.
I numbered all I could not do,
Saw it best not to write about you.

Poetry/Scott Stewart

Learning Goodbye

November days both.
The first relishing an autumn sun,
the second needles the skin with icy drizzle.
Unlike the first, with your family whirling and falling
out of the station wagon,
they are now loading the last luggage and stepping the dog
into the van.

We stand, kind'a looking at each other, kind'a not.

Your arm hooks mine. Our other arms
dangle,
forgetting
how to
hug.

Your
dad calls for you,
I sidle to the street, hands waving,
because there is nothing left to do.
My smile deepens as my eyes tighten . . .
Tightens and deepens . . . while the van
turns
at the end of the street
                    leaving two shallow honks
            to fall flat
    in a
tethered bounce

in the cold.
A foot in the gutter, one on the curb,
I stand. Looking, seeing nothing.
Waiting.
Wanting. Waiting
to feel the tears freeze on my face.

Poetry/Mary Jones

Warning

Right now,
they listen to you,
tell you they love you, bring you
bouquets of dandelions.

They tell you
what happened at school, what they
learned, who their friends are,
what they had for lunch.

They ask you
if you'll go with their class on a field trip,
if you'll take them to the zoo, the circus,
the playground.

Right now,
they need you to
take care of them—feed them,
clothe them, read to them,
guide them, answer their questions,
interpret the world.

And you have such
dreams for them—they'll be athletes,
musicians, rocket scientists.
They'll find a cure for cancer,
create dazzling works of art.

> > >

But someday soon,
without a backward glance,
they will shrug off the
burden of your expectations
as easily as they
would shed a jacket on a warm day.

They will laugh at your
warnings as they gallop off
into the future like frisky colts,
where they will learn things
you cannot teach them,
where they will go places
you cannot follow.
Just as you did years ago.

Fiction/*Honorable Mention*/Kathleen Lindstrom

Gold Bracelets

"You're so prrrretty."

That's high praise indeed coming from Millie, who tells it like it is, whether you want to hear her opinion or not.

Tonight, it's nice to hear.

Millie's been sitting on the bed watching me get ready since after five. There she is, all scrunched up and happy—that big loopy smile on her face, her mouth wide open, a bit of drool, dripping, delight in her eyes.

My biggest fan, I think to myself and start to smile. *A pain in the neck, but my biggest fan.*

I'm getting ready for the prom and can't believe this is actually happening. Two weeks ago, I had finally resigned myself to the fact I'd be staying home on this night of nights. The other option was going with a bunch of girls everyone clearly knew were *rejects.* I decided I'd rather stay home.

But then Jesse asked me out and that changed everything. I was tutoring him in algebra at the time, helping him figure out the formula for finding the distance between lines that increase exponentially to reach 375 millimeters. He wasn't getting it.

That's when he said, "Do you want to go to the prom with me?"

It confused me at first: "But you're going with Beverly Chapman."

"Yeah, we were. But her parents grounded her. She got caught smoking weed."

Jesse and Beverly had been going steady since sophomore year. They weren't the most popular or best-looking couple in school, but they were definitely a couple. Whenever you saw Jesse, you saw Beverly Chapman hanging onto him.

"Well, do you?"

"Sure," I heard myself reply.

Now here I am, putting on my prom dress—a long blue

gown with a halter top, trimmed with rhinestones. Mom and I found it in a consignment shop and it was the only one that fit. But it looks good on me, if I do say so myself. Dad told me it brings out the blue in my eyes, which reminded him of the blue bonnets growing on his old family farm. "They're beautiful and perfect," he'd told me, eyes watering. "Just like my little girl."

I'm tall and thin and tower over most of the boys at Shelby High, including Jesse—which I hate. So tonight I'll be wearing flats—which I also hate. As a final touch, I roll my mom's gold bracelets up my arms and pin a white orchid in my hair. Then I look in the mirror.

I like what I see.

Millie does too, because she's squealing and clapping her hands, like she does when Big Bird shows up on Sesame street. A good sign, I think, because Millie is a truth machine. She's eleven, but the doctors say she has the mind—and innocence—of a five-year-old.

That can be embarrassing sometimes, and that's when I want to pretend she belongs to someone else. Even taking her to the playground is an ordeal. Millie has a habit of greeting everyone she meets and telling them what she thinks. Now, when people see her coming, they cross the street, knowing what they're in for.

"Look, Nomi (my name is Naomi, but *Nomi* is as close as she gets), she's really fat," she'll say in her loud voice; or "That man walks funny," or "He smells like a fart."

I quit trying to shut her up years ago. Now I keep my eyes on the ground, pretending not to hear, refusing to acknowledge people's shocked faces, or the poor social skills of my little sister.

"Pretty, pretty, pretty," Millie claps, bouncing up and down, insisting I respond.

"Yes, Millie, I'm pretty. Thank you for telling me."

Millie starts playing with my gold bracelets, probably because she likes the clinking sound or the gleam of gold as they hit the light.

Mom says there's quite a story to these bracelets, which have been handed down to the oldest daughters in our family since World War II. In fact, Mom presented them to me as if she were turning over the Holy Grail.

She said they belonged to her Grandma Mary who fought for women's rights back when women didn't know they had any rights. She was jailed for picketing companies that wouldn't hire married women. Then she created a safe haven for battered wives—the first ever in the county. It mysteriously burned down in the middle of the night, however, due to faulty wiring—or so the police said. But Grandma Mary knew better. So she created another safe place, this time without revealing an address, which got her into more trouble.

"Grandma Mary was *fierce*," Mom told me. "She'd come back from these setbacks twice as strong. Nothing or no one kept her down for long."

In fact, she was arrested (and released) several times, proudly framing one of her mug shots (which my mother still has) showing a resolute woman with piercing blue eyes, daring anyone to get in her way.

I see it's already seven and Jesse will be here any minute. So Millie and I go downstairs, where I endure the *oohs* and *aahs* of my smiling parents. I sit on a hard chair, careful not to wrinkle my dress. I try to concentrate on TV, where contestants on *Wheel of Fortune* can't figure out that the answer on the board is Beauty and the Beast of Burden. It's so easy. But I'm too excited to really care.

At a quarter to eight, the phone rings and Mom answers. Just by watching her expression, I know what the conversation is all about. I brace myself for what's coming.

Mom ends the call with a frown and pursed lips, as taut as a coiled wire. She shakes her head back and forth, takes off her glasses, and rubs her eyes. Then she looks at me and sighs.

"Honey," she begins.

I look over at Millie, who looks scared, as if she knows what's coming.

It seems Beverly Chapman's parents decided to let her go to the prom at the last minute. Jesse picked her up twenty minutes ago and they're on their way to the gym. That was his mother, and she's so sorry. She's so ashamed of what her son has done. She's tried to raise him better than this.

My dad rises from the couch and goes into the kitchen. Mom just sits there, looking sad, wondering what more she can say. I'm running the gold bracelets up and down my arm, finding some strange comfort in their cold metallic feel.

I get up and head for the stairs. Millie follows.

In my room, I rip off the gown, roll it up and throw it in the back of my closet. I unpin my hair and mash the orchid into the floor until it looks like a big white stain.

"Good!" Millie says.

I put on pajamas and sit cross-legged on the floor, my head in my hands. Millie sits next to me. She slaps me on the back and says, "It's okay, Nomi. You'll be okay."

That's when I start to cry. I'm feeling ugly and useless and unwanted and so humiliated and ashamed. How can I ever face Jesse again, or even go back to school? The feelings are overwhelming and the tears come from someplace deep inside. Millie keeps patting my back.

But pretty soon, my tears turn into hiccups and the hiccups are exhausting. Now I'm tired and just want to sleep.

"I need to sleep, Millie. You better go now."

"You'll be okay, Nomi." She lays her head on my shoulder.

We sit on the floor in silence for a while. I hear Dad's van leaving the house, screeching down the road toward the freeway.

I put my arms around Millie and our foreheads touch. "You're such a wonderful girl," I tell her. "You are my best friend and I love you so much. I'm so glad you're my sister."

"Yah," Millie says, which makes me smile.

Millie continues playing with the bracelets on my arm.

"Fierce!" she tells me.

"Yeah," I respond, kissing her cheek. "We are."

Poetry/Jan Chronister

Station Wagon on a Friday Afternoon

On the backseat floor
paper bag holds
candy from the dime store,
suckers, jawbreakers, licorice whips.

In the front seat Mom sleeps
worn out from packing.
Dad mentally checks off
a list he worked on all week.

Neither one acknowledges
three squirming bodies
never getting comfortable
on the four-hour drive to the cabin.

I don't open my stash,
save sweetness for the week ahead.

Poetry/Thomas C. Stetzler

Saturday

The night is gone
as though it never was.
I wake to hear you humming
In the kitchen,
the coffee perking
as you set out the cups.

In the early light
we take our coffee
on the porch,
sharing quiet words,
low laughter,
as though someone
sleeping could hear.

An old dog rises,
moves into the sun,
plops back down.

And so the hours pass
like a slow-moving river
winding on until
it is out of sight.

Creative Nonfiction/Marlys Guimaraes

Meditation 101

"Breathe. Close your eyes. Feel the air moving in and out of your chest. Quiet your thoughts. Breathe."

The monk's brown robes flowed in folds around his crossed legs and sandaled feet. His voice slid over the audience in waves, caressing the minds of beginner meditation students.

In and out, I thought. *Breathing in—and—out.* I practiced the technique, despite consuming worries about my daughter, pregnant with twins, and on bed rest.

"When thoughts come, don't fight them; just let them go," he said.

My mind repeated the mantra. *Breathe, all is well, all will be well, breathe.* My limbs softened. I was getting into the zone, the one where you feel you are being rocked in the arms of a loving mother. Soft. Protected.

But then I peeked. All around me, participants sat cross-legged, hands on their knees. My legs stuck straight out, feet pointed to the ceiling like Tin Man in *The Wizard of Oz.* I tried to cross them under me. The pain was so severe that I heard a groan leave my throat and vibrate around the silent room. I was horrified.

"Don't worry about meditating correctly," he said. "Just breathe. This is a time to rest your mind, let your cares go, concentrate on your breath, in and out, deeper, slower, relax into the stillness."

I returned to the stickman position and followed his directives, letting go of my embarrassment, my worries about the upcoming birth, and breathed in and out. On the out breath, I let go of stress and on the in breath, I breathed in calm.

Yes, I thought, *this is just what I need.* I felt the clench in my stomach dissipate and my jaw muscles loosen. I didn't care that my mouth slacked open, saliva threatening to spill.

My cellphone vibrated.

In the vault-like quiet, it was as clear as a fire alarm. I peeked at the monk. He didn't move. I stepped out to take the call, breathing in and out, in and out, recalling his words: "All phones must be turned off during the session."

What would he know about having a daughter facing premature labor? I rationalized.

I returned to my spot on the floor, relieved that she was fine, and continued the breathing concentration. But I worried. *Was the monk angry?* I couldn't relax; fear of being offensive stuck to me.

The monk spoke. He instructed the group to stand and walk, clasp hands behind their backs, and study each step—a slow, walking mediation.

I followed close behind him as we walked around the room, hoping his calm would fog me and I would return to mindfulness. When my Nikes wanted to speed-walk past his turtle pace, I stared at my feet and willed them to behave.

Anxiety loosened its grip and once again my muscles relaxed as I contemplated each touch of heel and toe to the floor. When the class ended, I was drenched in calm tranquility, ready to face the trip ahead of me into rush hour traffic to a distant hospital and a waiting daughter.

I walked out of the class to my car, continuing the walking meditation. The leaves on the trees were vibrant, the sidewalk a smooth river of peace, my car a shimmering silver cloud. Lungs expanded as I drew in cool rain-washed air.

I reached into my purse for keys. I dug deeper. Deeper still. My breath increased, my heart raced. I dumped the purse contents onto the moist ground. Bits of stone and gravel dug into my knees as I pawed through pens, lipsticks, Post-it notes, and charge cards. Coins rolled under the car and crinkled receipts fluttered into the air.

I looked up to see the monk pass by me, a slight smile at the corner of his lips.

I stuffed the contents of my purse back into its pouches, left pennies on the ground for luck, and ran back to the classroom.

Nothing.

Up and down stairs I flew, checking the bathroom and the gift shop. Anxiety reached its apex, heading toward volcanic dimensions.

When I found the keys, turned into security by a kind person, I ran to my car and drove down the road, jaw tight, hands clenched to the steering wheel, my car a blazing speeding chariot.

Poetry/Michael Kiesow Moore

Inside the Stone

It is warm inside this black stone.
The lava from earth's deeps still heats.
Off to the left is a tunnel there.
Follow it down, down, down,
where darkness is hotter than a star,
and light is so black you can
see where time begins.
We are all like this inside,
filled with the Old Light
waiting to return home.

Poetry/Micki Blenkush

Fort of Ice and Snow

Warm days after so much snow
invited industry.
My daughter left boulders
high as her fourth-grade
          shoulders
strewn about the field
like a midwest Stonehenge
until on the weekend
her father helped to move them
all together.

Her dream of a simple tunnel
widened to a room-sized fort
complete with salvaged wood
for shelves and a sturdy roof
to protect from birds of prey
when they pretended as mice
to shape morsels for their larder.
I could barely see their outlines
when I called them in from
          foggy dusk.

At first light we saw the trampled
          pile.
Footprints around crushed ruin.
Shelves stabbed into snow
like relics from a razed temple
in a torn land.

To have no balm for her
          mourning.
No answers to who and why.
Only the what of collapse
by someone who'd watched
before night arrived
to blanket the field.

What prayer might we offer
such willful destruction?
I speak of sun and melt
as she plans
to build again.

Fiction/Jennifer Hernandez

Tarot: Strength

She could feel the roar building inside her chest. The boys were bickering again in the next room. For the millionth time that day. Over minutiae as always. Mostly questions of whose feet were touching whom, as they insisted on waging constant turf battles on the couch, leaving the two recliners to the cats. Why couldn't they just get along? Or, save that, why couldn't they just keep it down? Her nerves couldn't take much more.

Then the explosion. One's foot knocked over the other's drink. Shrieks ensued as he-of-the-spilled-drink clobbered the drink-spiller to the floor and began to pummel him. She leapt from her perch in the kitchen and grabbed the pummeler by the collar, trying to haul him off his brother, bellowing all the while, "Stop! Get off him!"

She had begun practicing yoga, even walking meditation of a sort, as she carried laundry baskets up and down the stairs of the split level. When would the serenity kick in? When would she achieve balance? She was waiting for the day that she could glide into the room, chestnut locks floating behind her, infinity crown neatly in place, and with a gesture—or at most a calm word—tame the lions, both those within her and those without.

In the meantime, she pried her older son off his brother, with no small effort on her part, banished him to his room, and promised herself to add weight training to her regimen ASAP.

Poetry/Susan Niemela Vollmer

Cousins

We had cousins then of just the right ages
Not the perfectly coiffed ones
We greet now with artificial hugs
But real cousins who knew the names of our dolls
And all the best places to spy on our brothers

Cousins who figured out how to sneak into Grandpa's attic
And whose mom always had a cookie for us
Cousins good for an argument over whether to play
Catalog paper dolls, endless games of Monopoly
Or drive a wagon train around the basement

They were cousins who sang as tunelessly as we did
And who enjoyed the old camp songs just as much
We swung higher and higher on the backyard swings
Kicked our shoes off into the raspberry patch
And believed that we would always travel side by side

Creative Nonfiction/Kim A. Larson

Code Jordan

Seconds. That's all it took—and he was gone.

While waiting in a check-out lane at Walmart, my three-year-old son Jordan begged for a treat. Who could blame him, tempted by rows of eye-level candy? Ignoring his pleas, I unloaded my cart. At the next glance, he was missing.

My stomach dropped as I fought off full-fledged panic. Surely he was nearby, the candy always sweeter in another lane. I raced through the check-out area calling his name, my knees threatening to give out. Where could he be? Had he been abducted?

It was a parent's worst nightmare, and the missing-child protocol, Code Adam, wasn't yet in place. It wouldn't be activated until a year later, in 1994. Created by Walmart, the protocol was named in honor of Adam Walsh, the abducted and murdered son of John Walsh—who later hosted the television series *America's Most Wanted*.

Near tears, I implored a store clerk for help. She paged the store manager, and within minutes I was describing my energetic, adorable, blonde-haired, blue-eyed son. She radioed his description to her employees and asked their help. How could I live if anything happened to him? Why hadn't I been watching him better?

Adrenaline short-circuited my ability to think. What should I do? I called Jordan's name, wandering. The manager reined me in. Someone would find him, she reassured me, and Jordan would need me when they did.

Several minutes later she received a call from a clerk in the women's department. Someone had found him hiding in the middle of a circular clothing rack. I ran to his location, and we both burst into tears upon being reunited.

That wasn't the first time Jordan went missing, nor would it be the last.

Like most children, Jordan loved to play outside. Our house was at the end of a quiet cul-de-sac, and our fenced backyard adjoined other neighbors. It should have been a safe haven for him.

One summer evening, I let him loose in the backyard while I cleaned up after supper. This was before the Walmart scare, so he wasn't yet three at the time. Every few minutes I glanced out the kitchen window or patio door to check on him. The last time I did, I couldn't see him anywhere.

I ran outside calling his name and searched every inch of ground. How could a two-year-old disappear from inside a fenced yard? He wasn't tall enough to reach the latch, which I had secured earlier. I raced to the front yard. My husband was visiting with several neighbors, and they hadn't seen Jordan either.

We formed a search party and began knocking on doors, yet no one had seen him. We were about to call the police when our next-door neighbor, who'd been helping with the search, came rushing out of his house. He had gone inside for a minute and found Jordan in their family room.

Jordan told us he had climbed over the fence and let himself in. All that time he had been watching cartoons with a boy his age.

Though the police weren't called that time, they would be the next.

It happened two summers later at the home of our wonderful daycare provider, Julie. Jordan and the other children were playing outside when she asked them to pick up their toys before lunch. Busy in the kitchen, she kept an eye on them from her window. When routinely counting heads, she came up short—one boy short.

With her ability to search impeded by a houseful of children, she called the police. Armed with his physical description and our home address, the officers set out to find him. It wasn't long before they located him eight blocks away, playing in his sandbox at home.

Spared the drama until I picked him up, I heard the whole story, often told in first person, as Jordan proudly displayed the police-badge sticker stuck to his shirt. "They gave me this, too." He grinned, handing me a coupon for free French fries at Hardees. What kind of deterrent was that? The police should have handcuffed him. Roughed him up a bit. Though he probably would have enjoyed that too.

French fries? Give me a break. No, he deserved to be grounded—indefinitely. Or at least until he could start hockey. His exuberant energy needed a full-throttle-sport outlet.

That fall he began his hockey career. Besides the enrollment fees, each family was required to raise additional funds by selling Christmas wreaths. Our little rookie could hardly wait to hit up our neighbors to support his new venture.

The next morning when it was time to leave home, Jordan didn't answer my calls. Finding his coat missing, I assumed he was outside playing in the snow. A quick glance around our yard proved me wrong. The streetlights were dimming on our sleepy street, the sun peeking over the horizon. A house light flickered at the end of the block, and an outline of two figures could be seen inside the front entry. As I approached the house, Jordan bounced outside, beaming. He had made his first sale.

I scolded him for worrying me.

"I told you I was going to sell wreaths," he said. "You must not have been listening." How many times had I said that to *him*? He hopped into the car, excited to make his next sale with Julie.

As Jordan got older, I continued to struggle with losing him. Like when he left home for college, or traveled to Sweden, or got his first real job. Now, at twenty-five, he's applied for a job transfer to London—England! To him, life is still an adventure.

To me, motherhood has happily been adventure enough.

Poetry/Kristin Laurel

Jesus, It's Nearly Christmas

What am I doing at the mall?
It's been a hell of a year, and my kids want
new i-Pads. I'll show them i-Care;
it's what good, divorced mothers do

for atonement. For leaving their father,
for the death of their cousins, their grandpa,
for all the bad days at school, this year
and the years to come.

I carry the weight of motherhood
like the roof of the old, worn-out Metrodome
that collapsed from too much snow,
too much heaviness.

This December, it's so damn cold,
my eyeballs and my heart feel frozen.
But then the cashier at Holiday gives me free hot chocolate,
I go home and find a neighbor's plowed the driveway;

my marrow turns soft, my bones leak love.
I snap apart a piece of peanut brittle.

Poetry/*Reprinted from *Talking Stick 4, 1997*/ Deane Johnson

Sand Sculpture

Tiny feet patter along the wet, firm beach
That the tide has left behind. They stop,
Turn, sink in just a bit.
He stares as she begins to dig.

Her hands work the fresh, wet sand,
As the long mound forms beneath them.
Shaped into curves with gentle smoothes and pats,
It grows a tail, a head, a nose, and feet.

More feet arrive, with a brown-eyed boy,
A girl, then two, then three.
They watch shyly at first, then approach,
Eager to stuff the body of the beast.

A serpent grows beneath their hands,
Long and brown, it whips its tail of sand.
Surrounded now by a sea of small feet,
It is pushed, prodded, patted to life.

Scales now form across its back and tail.
Claws appear one by one, to grasp
The sand, to cling, to fight the tide
That licks its hungry way back up the shore.

Even as its eyes are finally opened,
As it turns its head to see the wonder
Fixed in eyes all around, its tail flicks the water,
Feels the cool touch of oblivion.

> > >

Even as its tail is melted away,
Swept before the relentless surf,
As its eyes splash to sand before the sea,
eyes gleam in delight, laugh in fear.

Icy waves slap at ankles, scatter the feet
which tear up the seafloor in a rush for safety.
They fly up the beach amid squeals and shouts,
Eyes yet laughing.

Poetry/Mary A. Conrad

Haiku

serene pools conceal
craters where cliffs confronted
lashing wind and waves

Poetry/Charmaine Pappas Donovan

Mimicking Sparrows

They swoop across highways,
shape-changing over field stubble,
where crops no longer green
leafy rows in fertile ground.
Their flock grows round,
then skinny and string-like,
undulates higher, shifts and slides
like a ladder slanting
toward the ground.

What guides this swarm
—how do birds flock—
dancing dark designs
onto today's bright blue sky?
What keeps sparrows from colliding
as they careen through space?
Each feathered wing-flap
adjusts in the blink of an eye,
in milliseconds of graceful precision.

We, too, learn to keep
a safe distance
between us,
sometimes colliding,
falling to the ground.
But when we flow
like the sparrows
we, too, travel the skies.
At arm's length, we dance
like birds made for each other.

Poetry/Sister Rafael Tilton, OSF

Pilgrim, the Path

One more snow walk.
After yesterday's drizzle of sleet,
I test each step's push
against a crusty glaze that holds
seven-eighths of my weight.
Each break-through
jars my very skull.
My heels hit hard on the ridges
of yesterday's toe holes.
Frozen now,
sharp flanges of slush
bark my shins at every step.
Squinting, as white hot sunfire
glances off frost mounds,

Pilgrim,
I see,
the path is *not*
made by walking.
No. By slipping,
falling to one's knees,
sliding off the humps,
skidding, stumbling,
stomping,
groping for footholds,
furrowing,
retracing,
diving through,
plowing through,
looking back in April
to see an erratic,
zigzag, drunken
determination
threaded across the green.

Creative Nonfiction/Bonnie West

She Was a Woman Who

The quote arrived in my email from a friend who liked to send thoughts for the day. *She was a woman who, between courses, could be graceful with her elbows on the table.*—Henry James (1843 -1916)

Could it possibly be, my friend was implying I lacked grace?

I thought about the woman, a woman who could be graceful with her elbows on the table, while sitting in a coffee shop with *my* elbows on the table and a slight scent, from what I assumed I hadn't completely scraped off the bottom of my sandal, mixing with the aromatic Costa Rican blend.

Whatever happened to women like her, in the time of Henry James?

I contemplated the thought while I blew across the coffee cup. Some milky froth splashed onto my keyboard so I stood up fast to grab a napkin and, in my hurry, knocked my cinnamon scone onto the floor. I grabbed it, almost before it hit the ground, and set it back on the plate, and knew I was not a woman who, between courses, could be graceful with her elbows on the table.

When I'd ordered my coffee I'd asked for "a real cup," and the woman answered in a snotty tone, "All of our cups are real." I was nonplussed, or was it not nonplussed? What I was, in the end, was pissed. I was annoyed at not having thought of the word "mug" right off the bat and having had to say, "not paper," and then I was irritated by her show of attitude, and finally I was pissed that I didn't know the exact meaning of the word "nonplussed." Then I'd returned to the table and my computer, set down the coffee and scone and, after spilling and dropping and finally getting over the nasty barista, continued to think about Henry James and that woman.

I wasn't the kind of woman who, between courses, could be

graceful with her elbows on the table. I talked loudly and too fast and I laughed like a donkey. I felt compelled to tell everybody, even strangers who did not want to hear, all the things I found funny or stupid or clever, whether those things were, or were not. I imposed my political and religious opinions on even the gentlest humanity. I spoke of sex inappropriately. And since I'd entered the coffee shop, I had mentally used the words *dog-shit, snotty, fuck, bitch, pissed*, and couldn't remember the definition of a simple word. A woman who, between courses, could be graceful with her elbows on the table, didn't think the words *fuck* or *pissed* and, needless to say, could define *nonplussed*.

I wasn't familiar with this particular heroine. Was she a main character in one of his novels? Was she young? Was she old? Was she a character at all? Perhaps she was his wife, illicit lover or friend. (I had no idea, did Henry James take lovers? Did I care?) The only thing I knew for certain, character or lover, was, I was nothing like this woman.

I had read Henry James long ago, and now, I knew as completely as I knew I was not she, that a woman who could be graceful with her elbows on the table, would have read and remembered the heroines of Henry James.

And perhaps while she sat at the table being graceful and no doubt attentive to the gentleman or gentlewoman beside her, she may have taken her hand out of her lap, rested her delicate chin in her soft palm and left her elbow on the table and, with her small white teeth exposed just a bit behind her lips, she might have mentioned a novel she'd just enjoyed written by a man called Herman Melville, Stephen Crane, or Henry James. She might have asked those around her if they took pleasure in reading, making certain to give a gracious way out if they seemed unfamiliar with the author she had mentioned. She never would have quizzed them, hoping they might be caught out in their ignorance. She never would have said to the portly woman nervously blinking and nodding, "What exactly have you read?" She would have been incapable of placing her tablemates in a situation where they'd have to admit to not having read Melville or Crane or James. A woman who, between courses, could be graceful with her elbows on the table would never embarrass people, nor would she be willing to eat food from the same floor that a person in dirty sandals had stepped on, moments before.

I thought about how one message in an email had created in me thoughts and the pursuit of those thoughts, and I was about to wake up my computer and type in *Henry James* when I realized that she, this woman, never would have googled information any more than she would have put her feet up on the chair across from her or said the words *snotty* or *shit*. This woman would have treasured books, would have treated learning with dignity, would have appreciated the fact that she was allowed (yes, allowed!) to learn, and would have acknowledged by her behavior, how much had been sacrificed by unknown women who came before. She would have delighted in her books, those she borrowed, received as gifts or purchased. And I thought about the seldom used white card in my wallet and I thought yes, perhaps I would walk across the street and down two blocks to the library and check out Henry James (would that I could actually borrow the man himself!) and this time, I might just learn something from his writing, and although I knew I would fail at becoming that woman, that woman who began all this, I knew I could become a woman who was *trying* to be the kind of woman who, between courses, could be graceful with her elbows on the table.

Creative Nonfiction/*Reprinted from Talking Stick 13, 2004/*
Linda Henry

My Fleeting Firstborn   ✱

I imagine she is almost twelve now, and sitting next to me on the front stoop. She's a skinny-legged blonde, although that is as much as I can conjure.

"Do you ever wish you were here, with us, in this family?"

Always, she answers.

"Is it okay for us to talk this way? Doesn't God disapprove?"

It is not always possible. It is neither right nor wrong.

This feels like a Ouija board where I suspect I am subconsciously pushing toward the letters that will spell out what I want to hear. But I cannot stop.

"How am I doing? What do you see?"

You're really growing up, she says.

I laugh. "You're not."

I don't need to, she says matter-of-factly, which strikes me as impertinent.

I let her go, back to wherever she is, back to God. When I see her next, she may be fifteen months or fifteen years; I don't know how it works. It occurs to me that I'll have all eternity to get to know my firstborn. I smile, inhale the crabapple that is so gorgeous, so briefly in bloom, and go back inside the house, back to the living.

Poetry/Sandra Sidman Larson

Sheets

I heard the garbage collectors/scrambling at their work
 —from "Thinking of Winter in the Middle of July" by Carol Rucks
   (used with permission)

As I'm throwing away all my old journals,
I hear the garbage collectors scrambling at their work.

Words are hard to bury but they do decay.
I have a strategy to hold them still at night,

listen to them breathe. In the utter darkness
the stars have little to add, but they have

traveled millions of light years
to appear at the window, so why

shouldn't I talk with them? What is worth
remembering is best kept in bed.

Poetry/Stephanie Brown

Where To Go When There's Work To Do

The space beneath
      this pine foot stool—unremarkable
except for the cone-shaped
          sawdust pile.

Important work,
      disguised as rest, is going on unseen,
done in the dark galleries
          of our marrow.

Survival—mine,
      the carpenter ants, yours too—
depends on burrowing deeper
          to do our work.

Fiction/*Honorable Mention*/Chet Corey

The Rehearsal

The lightning, then the thunder. That was the sequence she repeated to herself as she stood looking out of the parlor window across field without windbreak all of the way to the Iowa line. Only the light from the cell tower was visible in cloudbank that seemed to drape onto their field like table linen from ironing board to floor.

He had died before planting had even begun. He'd turned up the field and laid it over upon itself, as he'd done each season on land inherited from his father, as his had from his. But that would be the end of it, with no children of their own to pass hand to hand to. They'd known that and had agreed upon it.

That was his favorite part of the planting season: preparing the fields. Once he'd compared it to foreplay. She remembered that and always would. He'd been no poet with words, but she recalled how he'd smiled after he'd said it. Now she smiled back at her seventy-four-year-old self reflected in windowpane, remembering how she'd blushed and how he'd said it gave her a delicate color, like the pink of prairie rose petals he'd seen by the outcropping of granite in the southwest corner of field.

Then thunder turned her from her own face in the windowpane to beyond the field. She'd missed the lightning, but heard its applause. Lightning, claps of thunder, and then that sound like a freight train blasting its air horns. That was the sequence that would send them to the fieldstone cellar with its dank dark as its overhead light bulb flickered out. They'd wait in that unholy dark, aware of each other's damp sweat, saying nothing, listening, conserving energy, as he would batteries in the flashlight he'd kept since childhood on a shelf among canning jars his mother put up—pickled or un-pickled—as she herself had afterwards. And always the over-sweet aroma of apples in the barrel, Macintosh and a few crab.

She knew where the flashlight was if she took to the cellar. But she stood her ground, immovable as the black walnut hutch beneath Da Vinci's *Last Supper*.

She would not go down—take to the cellar. She had decided upon it, and the decision had come so easily to her, as if a solution to a simple mathematics problem. She was good at that—figures, keeping records, managing the budget, buoying them up and out of bankruptcy in lean years. He at the fields, she at keeping book. They were a pair, though scuffed with wear, like his work boots, left in the mud room as he'd taken them off, neither toe pointing the same direction.

Everyone in town would think she'd simply got caught up by the suddenness of it all—had not heard the storm's approach. Perhaps they'd find her out in the field. That would be all right with her. He'd turned that field, like she'd turn back their bed. She'd rest comfortably awhile in its pillowed topsoil. Then they'd find her and lay her with him. Neighbors would be shocked and sad. It would make the weekly paper. The ladies would say it was meant to be, her husband in the ground less than a month. The men would shake their heads, get up and go out on the stoop for a smoke or busy themselves at some cleanup to be done in the aftermath of storm.

That was the sequence. The thunder, the lightning, and then the shudder like a freight at a crossing. But that runaway freight of a storm did not cross the trestle and throttle down track. She went out on the front stoop, the rain coming down softly as Gregorian chant.

Then suddenly it stopped. And all was still. She looked at the clapboard siding—flaking, in need of paint. It would be good if the house and sheds came down in storm. They were not fit for much. Perhaps the rafters in the barn. They'd be salvaged, be of some use. The machinery had been sold off, and they'd willed the farm place and fields to sustain their parish grade school.

She'd forgotten about the quiet, the calm after the storm. She breathed in the wet earth air, his coal-black topsoil caught up in it. And she remembered how his body smelled of hard-earned sweat on days he'd return in the heat of noon and take her to bed.

There would be other storms. She wouldn't be anxious about it. This had been a rehearsal. And it had gone well. When another would come and another, she'd stand at the parlor window and count the seconds between lightning strike and thunderclap until the pitch-black cloud, with its tail like an Angus bull twitching before a heifer, touched down and switched it all away.

Poetry/Lane Rosenthal

Awake

The warm weight of a down quilt
presses against my body
like a lover
whose absence
fills the blue morning light,
and whispered velvet words are all
empty arms grasp.

Poetry/ *Reprinted from Talking Stick 12, 2003/*
Angele (Burlingame) Hartell

Revealed

Round bales of hay
Stand like scattered sentinels
In the deep mist of an evening
Disguised by dusk.
What are you waiting for?
Whom do you seek?

If I walk into the mist,
Lay my hand upon your side
And listen in the dark,
Will you speak to me
Of sunny days and butterflies
And birds aloft and hope
Crushed beneath the mower's blade?
Will I see, through the mist
And twine that binds each
Living creature through eternity,
All that you are and have yet to be?

Poetry/*Editor's Choice*/Margaret M. Marty

Dear Childhood Home:

As dawn breaks over the east field
a chorus of birds pecks at my brain
and Barney barks at a car going by,
arousing me from dreamland.

The lacy, yellowed curtains flutter
at the south second-story window
overlooking the apple orchard
where Daddy planted many varieties.

Waffles bake on Mama's wood cookstove,
coffee percolates, side pork sizzles—
the aroma wafts up the narrow stairs
to the bedroom shared with my two sisters.

The rickety screen door bangs shut
behind me as I run to the swing
on the gnarly old box elder in time
to wave to Buster, the milk truck driver.

Later little sis and I meander cow paths
along the gurgling, spring-fed creek,
daring one another to jump across
from stone to stone in shallow places.

We find newborn kittens in the haymow,
gently cradle them as they mew,
place them to their mother's teats,
then back away in awe and respect.

> > >

We run toward the chickens
to make them squawk and scatter,
gingerly avoid their droppings
as we walk barefoot back to the house.

Along the hedge of lilac bushes
we play house with our dolls,
wash their clothes, and Mama hangs them
on the line too high for us to reach.

No wonder I was drawn,
like a magnet that won't be denied,
to spend the remainder of my life
on this hallowed piece of earth.

Creative Nonfiction/Tarah L. Wolff

Old Farm Houses

They are a common sight along the dirt roads up here, almost always flanked by overgrown lilacs and a barn staggering to its knees in their shadows. Our state's old farm houses share many characteristics. They are usually around a hundred years old; they usually all started as white and many of them are still, stubbornly standing against the brutality of our Minnesota weather. Some haven't made it this long and my heart keeps note of them whether my mind consciously remembers them or not. I drive by, after having not been by here for months and, *Oh, that old girl's roof finally gave in.* Her boarded up windows and porch cocked across the front of her like a broken arm had not yet taken her with them. Until now. The long rot of a little hole becoming a bigger hole, is almost always the way it goes. A little moisture at a time, not even noticeable to the untrained eye for years, until it finally takes its toll and her death bell rings silently across the prairie.

I've been watching these old places since I was a kid and still have my favorites. Up on the Hubbard Prairie there is one that I'll never forget. The house is your typical Minnesota farmhouse, two-story, white clapboard siding with tall windows and a front porch. This one is one of my favorites because over a hundred feet of its flanking property on the road is a run of lilacs like I have never before seen. I've driven over ten miles out of my way, every day for two weeks, just to see them bloom. Windows rolled all the way down, I've taken two passes just to SMELL and I have no doubt if they noticed me they must have thought I was nuts. But, if the current owners had ever come out, I would have told them in complete sincerity, "Thank you for keeping the old place." And they have, not always very prettily, but they have kept the old place going; the house is still standing, still protecting people after so many years.

At first glance, there is a feeling of poverty here that they all seem to carry. A feeling of a life that started in excitement for the future, of richness and reward that slowly dwindled down to the reality of a life living off the dirt in a hard climate. A life totally dependent on a few months to produce enough to survive one more brutal winter. Animals, first gathered here in great number until the reality of the situation thinned the herd down to nothing. Now the barn, once standing full of life, echoes the coos of pigeons back to you, as there is nothing else living in them now. What once was a landscape of forest hiding the old farmsteads are now bare fields felled on the hope of one more acre providing just a little more income to prove the farming life worth it. Now most of them remain on a little corner of trees, all that's left to shield the farm house from the north wind but only if the "kids" haven't let them go yet to whatever massive farming company that now owns all the fields around them. If they have been let go, all that can be found of the life that was lived here is what might be a driveway access or a stray lilac bush, close enough to the road that it was left to remain. The rest buried beneath the plow.

They have not all been let to fall though. There are the "kids" that stayed, now silver-haired, still keeping the old house of their parents where they grew up. Few stayed in farming and few could afford to fix the big old barns for no other reason than pure nostalgia and respect for the awesome undertaking that it was to accomplish such a feat a hundred years ago. But, some have been saved and updated. When I drive by one of those old barns, sporting a fancy new steel roof, it's everything I can do to not stop and gush, "Oh, my gosh, look at you and your new roof!" And the same for the old farm houses, now sporting fancy new siding and looking ready for a first date with their new windows and paint.

Some of the grandkids did it too and I know this because I'm one of them. I was able to save my grandparents' old farm house and now, when I drive by all those old houses, I am comforted by the thought that saving one of them, just one, might not mean much to most people, but to me it means just about everything.

Creative Nonfiction/*Honorable Mention*/
Georgia A. Greeley

Recipes

She didn't just cook in her kitchen. My grandmother would look around and take notice. Whistle-humming through her teeth, always in an apron, she paid attention while she worked. On the Cinnamon Coffee Cake recipe she wrote, "Saw my first robin today." On the Rhubarb Sauce recipe, "The hollyhocks might not make it this year." On the Spritz recipe it still says, "Jimmie looked two inches taller as he walked through the door." It took over a year before Mom found the time to sort through my grandmother's recipe cards; she found her mother. In small deliberate notes. Daily details. Mom cried for two days while reading recipes. She let all those unexpected words feed her heart.

Poetry/Niomi Rohn Phillips

Snowbirds in Paradise

they were two generations removed
from Norway and the Ukraine
their grandparents' dreams
of freedom . . . fulfilled
and the frigid narrowness
of North Dakota
nurtured limited vision

they took sensible steps
into the world
college, marriage, children
in old-fashioned order
the harsh winters of their marriage
softened by spring birdsong
and sweet summers

they never envisioned
the wonder
of winter in Hawaii
where meadowlarks and doves
join them for endless summer

Fiction/Jim Russell

Lady Luck

Hi there, young man. Come on in.
Your first time here?
Relax, you'll have the time of your life.
I'll see to that.
Oh, I have so much to teach you—cards,
        craps, slots, the wheel.
Look, you've won something already!
And that's just the beginning.
Don't be a stranger now.

Hey, mister, long time no see.
Remember me? Say, didn't we have fun last time!
For a while anyway.
Tonight we can start all over again.
Sky's the limit.
You can bet your life on it!

Hello, old friend.
Yes, I'm still here.
That's right, we go back a long way together.
Come on, the game's the same.
Shall we give it another whirl for old time's sake?
That's right, ante up.
What have you got to lose?

How may I help you, madam?
A game of chance?
Oh, you're looking for someone?

> > >

Well, we get all kinds in here—fathers, sons, husbands.
What's that, no food on the table?
No money for the rent?
See here, don't blame me. Gambling was *his* idea.
Madam! Watch your language!
After all, *I am a lady*!

Creative Nonfiction/*Honorable Mention*/Mike Lein

The Perfect Crime

It was a dark and stormy night outside my cozy cabin. The inside temperature dropped as wind howled and snow rattled off windows. I got up from my chair and added another piece of hand-split, free-range, locally grown, organic, air-dried oak to the cheery blaze in the wood stove, then sat back down to the computer to ponder the perfect crime.

Last summer I ran short of firewood and started thinking about winter—winter without firewood and heat at my rustic weekend retreat. Without firewood there would be no ice fishing on Crooked Lake, no cross country skiing with the dog, no quiet nights with the wood stove warming my back as I wrote. It might drive a law-abiding man to a life of crime.

A fallen oak on neighboring property tempted me. The mighty trunk had splintered in a thunderstorm and sent the tree crashing down. It lay there on uninhabited foreclosed property, wasting away while legal matters were resolved in a faraway place. It was a victimless crime waiting to happen. And if there was a victim, it was me, since I had paid for years of snowplowing and gravel hauling on the shared driveway with no help from the vanished neighbor.

So, supposing I was ready to commit a misdeed in the name of warmth, how would I pull the caper off without ending up in the local jail—or at very least in the headlines of the local newspaper? It was more complicated than it sounds and, for all I know, firewood theft may be a capital offense here in the Northwoods, like stealing a horse in the Old West.

Logistics would be one problem. The tree was over two feet in diameter and lay fifty yards off the driveway in thick brush. It would need to be cut into manageable pieces and hauled out bit by bit. However, once done, the thick summer greenery would hide the crime scene for months. The new owners would never know it had been there.

Chainsaw noise was an obvious issue. No one has yet invented a stealth chainsaw. I'd have to choose my best saw, make sure it was full of gas and oil, get the dang thing to start, and then cut like crazy before someone investigated. I don't have many neighbors. But they are nosy, know the property lines, and might not be able to keep quiet.

Another threat might be a tourist from the resort down the road, out for a walk with a curious mutt. I could wear my camouflage hunting clothes and mask to hide from a walker. But some friendly Labrador or Golden Retriever might smell me and come crashing into the woods, tail wagging, happy to make a new friend. A camo-clad, masked guy wielding a chainsaw might look a little suspicious to the Master. That would make a headline in the local paper or at least a note in the police report.

There would be other dangers. Any crime show watcher knows that something is bound to go wrong. My saw could refuse to start, run out of gas, or get stuck in the tree at a critical moment. Any of those would be bad enough but the resulting swearing on my part could draw in those curious neighbors. Or maybe I would break a leg stepping in a woodchuck hole and have to call for help. Or even have the tree crush me in an unhandy moment. There's a headline for you—"Local Cabin Owner Flattened By Tree While Stealing Firewood." Also possible was that my old trailer would break an axle and leave a trailer load of purloined wood blocking the driveway for all to see.

Then there's the age-old problem of leaving evidence at the scene of the crime. It's not likely that local law enforcement would spend much time investigating this crime, even if it was reported. However, I have been known to lose things, even when not stressed out in the midst of questionable activity. A misplaced glove, a lost coffee cup, or a piece of broken trailer taillight might make solving this crime too easy and tempt them to haul me in just to pad year-end statistics. I'd have to be careful about loading the trailer too. A series of road-killed logs or leaking sawdust leaving a Hansel and Gretel style trail back to the cabin wouldn't be good.

My problems wouldn't end once the wood was back to my yard. More chainsaw work and the sweaty job of splitting the mess would take time. And speaking of nosy persons, my wife was bound to notice. "Where'd you get the wood?" she'd ask.

"Back in the woods," I'd answer evasively.

"Oh, when did you stop at the DNR office and get the firewood permit?" she would persist.

"I didn't, this is from private land—not the forest," I'd reply.

"Our land?" she might ask, again a bit too nosy for her own good.

"No," I'd say, voice dripping with sarcasm. "Not ours—the neighbors!"

Maybe that would get her to back off in time for me to finish splitting, stacking, and covering before anyone else showed up and started the same line of questioning. I'd hate to have to make someone "disappear" just to cover up the theft of a little firewood.

I got up and added another piece of hand-split, free-range, locally grown, organic, air-dried oak to the wood stove. Yes, this could be the perfect crime, especially once all the evidence has gone up in smoke.

Poetry/Bethany Bridge Hammer

The Burning Barrel

Shooting flames leapt like red-legged hoppers
in high grass, threatening the leafy-fingered
ash limbs dangling down,
and fire-cracked the burning barrel
one deep lightning split.

Unfazed, the large-lipped thing,
its mouth agape, set crackle popping,
blazing crazy as
a box of July rockets spark-lit
and flaming off to Mars.

Lift-off past, we craned our necks to peek,
and where the makings of the smoke
once were—sticks of wind-broke oak
and chips of elm—we glimpsed
a seeming pot of salsa roja,

Hissing, spitting, hot and smoky,
smoky like the charcoal fur of Jake the cat
whose lemon eyes
above his singed tuxedo ran
as he bolted for the pasture brook.

Poetry/Audrey Kletscher Helbling

Prairie Garden Memories

Prairie roots practicality prevailed
in my farmwife mother's garden
lying lake-sized next to an ocean of field corn.
Yet, between rows of vegetables, flourished
an island of sturdy zinnias and dainty bachelor buttons.
Unnecessary, but necessary to feed her soul.

Radishes emerged first in her planned plot,
tugged from the dirt like red bobbers
yanked from below the surface of the water.
The first catch of the season,
their zingy flavor nipped nostrils
with a pungent taste of spring.

Next to rows of radishes and lettuce,
green-topped onions waved in the wind,
buoys marking the garden patch.
We slid the slim slippery scallions
from damp soil, dipping the bulbs
into salt sprinkled on our palms.

Soon peas blossomed into pods,
as abundant as a school of crappies
multiplying in cool waters.
Filleted with the trace of a thumb,
shells split to reveal pearls of peas
strung in tasteful perfection.

> > >

With daylight stretching and sun shining strong,
the garden thrived, promising a good catch—
Monet flowers and a stringer of food for the table.
Kohlrabi. Bug-infested broccoli. Green beans.
Then milky corn and sun-ripened tomatoes.
Royal-hued eggplant and colorless cauliflower.

Later, bottom-feeding root crops—
carrots, parsnips and beets—matured
into trophy lengths worth measuring.
Sliced or diced, simmered or fried,
tubers filled our plates with vegetables
rooted deep in the land of our great-grandparents.

When the growing season waned, we unhooked
lunker squash and pumpkins from vines
and netted potatoes in burlap bags.
We sliced sumptuous melons tasting of summer,
juice trickling down chins, as we prepared
for winter on the frozen Minnesota prairie.

Poetry/Richard Fenton Sederstrom

Residuaries

We reside on the shore surrounding the lake.
We are held here between the forest and the lake
in residuary stasis while what changes, changes.

It's like the lake itself, the water held
for a geologic second in banks left behind
as residual debris by the last passing glacier.

The lake resides in its bed. Wet glacial residue.
The lake knows that it stays for only a little while,
part of it always seeping out or evaporating,

part of it replenished by rain, by the lakes
above it in its chain of glacial kettles, part by springs
swollen from inter-drought generosity.

The lake knows that someday it will either dry up
or it will overflow its banks somewhere and rejoin the flow
it has been only a stopover for these few flowing millennia.

But the lake doesn't care, doesn't need to care.
In whatever shape, in whatever place or places,
or whatever momentum, it is what it is.

Residuary here then, we take our dimensions
from the lake itself, our part of its space, our fate
to take part in *its* sense of time, and not our own.

Poetry/Tim J. Brennan

Under Earth

(i)
In southeastern Minnesota
bronzed men plow,
plant, furrow black earth
into rows as straight
as their lives

(ii)
Roger Waters was pulled
from his barn rafters
yesterday afternoon
Foreclosure,
they said
The noose still hangs
above the odor
of his black, now
fermenting beans

(iii)
In southeastern Minnesota
the wind rarely stops,
by instinct it is tolerated
It blows neighbors' dust
onto neighbors' clothes,
hung beneath neighbors' lines
that carry neighbors' voices
talking of another Friday fish fry,
a dance at the American Legion
or tomorrow night's movie being shown
on the Ace Hardware outside white wall

(iv)
Returning home late
on this two lane county highway,
it is cloudy and black
Farmyard lights look like tiny
        planets
in an earthen solar system
The AM radio crackles
from distant lightning
in your rearview mirror

Poetry/Laura L. Hansen

Danish Fiddler at Nisswa-stammen

Music flies off the strings of his violin
like sparks from an electrical wire
that has not been grounded.

His playing is muscular, energetic.
It moves like the dartdiphover
of a slightbright hummingbird.

It soars with wide strong raptor wings
as it dives down from the steep shelf
of the fjord.

The Dane appears young, might
in fact be a doppleganger to one
of my nephews.

His copper-blonde hair, cut short
and neat, gleams in the brief hot
Minnesota sun.

His fingers, on small square hands,
are lithe and agile, but look like
acceptable hands

for carpentry as well, or setting
a hook, or scaling a rock wall.
Worlds of work

might live in those hands
that scythe the fields of notes
and toss them up against the sun.

This is a good harvest, plentiful,
and to be celebrated.

"The talking stick is a Native American tradition used to facilitate an orderly discussion. The stick is made of wood, decorated with feathers or fur, beads or paint, or a combination of all. Usually speakers are arranged in a talking circle and the stick is passed from hand to hand as the discussion progresses. It encourages all to speak and allows each person to speak without interruption. The talking stick brings all natural elements together to guide and direct the talking circle." —Anne Dunn

This year, we received over 430 submissions from 266 writers. From these, the editorial board selected 139 poems, 26 creative nonfiction, and 20 fiction pieces from 118 writers for inclusion in this volume. Also, this year, we have reprinted 9 previously published items from 9 of the earlier JWB members who formed the group many years ago.

Please submit again!

www.thetalkingstick.com
www.jackpinewriters.com

Contributors

Without the following contributors, this Talking Stick would not have been possible. Thank you to everyone!

Benefactors
Kathryn Knudson
Sonja Kosler
Harlan and Marlene Stoehr

Special Friends Single
Sue Reed Crouse
Cindy Fox
Paisley Kauffmann
Mike Lein
Shasha Porter
Penny Westfall

Good Friends Couple
Jan and Joe Braun
Larry and Peggy Nelson

Good Friends Single
Stephanie Brown
Eric Chandler
Margaret M. Marty
Susan McMillen
Vincent D. O'Connor
Peter Stein

Friends Single
Chet Corey
Jennifer Hernandez
Ronald j. Palmer
William Upjohn
Susan Niemela Vollmer

Author List

Pagyn Alexander
Lina Belar
James Bettendorf
Micki Blenkush
Nicole Borg
Beth Diane Bradley
Janice Larson Braun
Tim J. Brennan
Stephanie Brown
Sue Bruns
Sandra Melchisedech Burwell
Eric Chandler
Sharon Chmielarz
Jan Chronister
Mary A. Conrad
Chet Corey
Susan Coultrap-McQuin
Sue Reed Crouse
Frances Ann Crowley
Zach Czaia
Joni L. Danzl
Nancy Devine
Charmaine Pappas Donovan
Cynthia Ekren
Larry Ellingson
Jeanne Emrich
Shirley Ensrud
Jeanne A. Everhart
Edis Flowerday
Cindy Fox
Mike Gainor
Carson T. Gardner

Shelley Getten
Katie Gilbertson
Georgia A. Greeley
Marlys Guimaraes
Kari E. Hagstrom
Bethany Bridge Hammer
Laura L. Hansen
Sharon Harris
Angele (Burlingame) Hartell
Audrey Kletscher Helbling
Linda Henry
Jennifer Hernandez
Sandra Howlett
Susu Jeffrey
Jennifer Jesseph
Arnie Johanson
Charles Johnson
Deane Johnson
Sawyer Johnson
Mary Jones
Meridel Kahl
James Robert Kane
Mary Christine Kane
Karen Kasland
Paisley Kauffmann
Ryan W. Keller
P. Helen Kester
Romayne Kilde
Norma Thorstad Knapp
Kathryn Knudson
Sonja Kosler
Kim A. Larson

Author List

Sandra Sidman Larson
Kristin Laurel
Mike Lein
Kathleen Lindstrom
Gail Lipe
Dawn Loeffler
Linda Maki
Cheyenne Marco
Margaret M. Marty
Michael McCormick
Susan McMillan
Kathryn Medellin
Jerry Mevissen
René Bartlett Montgomery
Michael Kiesow Moore
Ryan M. Neely
Joni Norby
David Eric Northington
Ronald j. Palmer
Yvonne Pearson
Susan Perala-Dewey
Kathleen Pettit
Niomi Rohn Phillips
Adrian S. Potter
Rebecca Ramsden
Deborah Rasmussen
Amy C. Rea
Kit Rohrbach
Lane Rosenthal
Jim Russell
Katherine Schaefer

Deb Schlueter
Mary Schmidt
Ruth M. Schmidt-Baeumler
Larry Schug
Richard Fenton Sederstrom
Candace Simar
Peter Stein
Doris Lueth Stengel
Thomas C. Stetzler
Scott Stewart
Harlan Stoehr
Marlene Mattila Stoehr
Sister Rafael Tilton, OSF
Mark Traynor
Peggy Trojan
Karen Turner
William Upjohn
Joel Van Valin
Rosemary Vaughn
Steven R. Vogel
Susan Niemela Vollmer
Justin Watkins
Miriam Weinstein
Bonnie West
Cheryl Weibye Wilke
Florence Witkop
Eric Wolff
Tarah L. Wolff
Cathy Ann Wood
Marie Zhuikov

www.ingramcontent.com/pod-product-compliance
Lightning Source LLC
Chambersburg PA
CBHW062111170626
46813CB00002B/399